LUCENT LIBRARY OF
**BLACK HISTORY**

# AFRICAN AMERICANS
# IN **POLITICAL OFFICE**
## From the Civil War to the White House

By Barbara M. Linde

Portions of this book originally appeared in
*Blacks in Political Office* by Michael V. Uschan.

**LUCENT**
P R E S S

Published in 2018 by
**Lucent Press, an Imprint of Greenhaven Publishing, LLC**
353 3rd Avenue
Suite 255
New York, NY 10010

Designer: Deanna Paternostro
Editor: Siyavush Saidian

**Library of Congress Cataloging-in-Publication Data**

Names: Linde, Barbara M.
Title: African Americans in political office: from the Civil War to the White House / Barbara M. Linde.
Description: New York : Lucent Press, 2018. | Series: Lucent library of black history | Includes index.
Identifiers: ISBN 9781534560758 (library bound) | ISBN 9781534560765 (ebook)
Subjects: LCSH: African Americans–Politics and government–Juvenile literature. | African Americans–
History–Juvenile literature.
Classification: LCC E185.6 L56 2018 | DDC 973'.0496073–dc23

Printed in the United States of America

CPSIA compliance information: Batch #BS17KL: For further information contact Greenhaven Publishing LLC, New York, New York at 1-844-317-7404.

Please visit our website, www.greenhavenpublishing.com. For a free color catalog of all our
high-quality books, call toll free 1-844-317-7404 or fax 1-844-317-7405.

# CONTENTS

# FOREWORD

Black men and women in the United States have become successful in every field, but they have faced incredible challenges while striving for that success. They have overcome racial barriers, violent prejudice, and hostility on every side, all while continuing to advance technology, literature, the arts, and much more.

From medicine and law to sports and literature, African Americans have come to excel in every industry. However, the story of African Americans has often been one of prejudice and persecution. More than 300 years ago, Africans were taken in chains from their home and enslaved to work for the earliest American settlers. They suffered for more than two centuries under the brutal oppression of their owners, until the outbreak of the American Civil War in 1861. After the dust settled four years later and thousands of Americans—both black and white—had died in combat, slavery in the United States had been legally abolished. By the turn of the 20th century, with the help of the 13th, 14th, and 15th Amendments to the U.S. Constitution, African American men had finally won significant battles for the basic rights of citizenship. Then, with the passage of the groundbreaking Civil Rights Act of 1964, many people of all races began to believe that America was finally ready to start moving toward a more equal future.

These triumphs of human equality were achieved with help from brave social activists such as Frederick Douglass, Martin Luther King Jr., and Maya Angelou. They all experienced racial prejudice in their lifetimes and fought by writing, speaking, and peacefully acting against it. By exposing the suffering of the black community, they brought the United States together to try and remedy centuries' worth of wrongdoing. Today, it is important to learn about the history of African Americans and their experiences in modern America in order to work toward healing the divide that still exists in the United States. This series aims to give readers a deeper appreciation for and understanding of a part of the American story that is often left untold.

Even before the legal emancipation of slaves, black culture was thriving despite many attempts to suppress it. From the 1600s to 1800s, slaves developed their own cultural perspective. From music, to language, to art, slaves began cultivating an identity that was completely unique. Soon after these slaves were granted citizenship and were integrated into American society, African American culture burst into the mainstream. New generations of authors, scholars, painters, and singers were born, and they spread an appreciation for black culture across America and the entire world. Studying the contributions of these talented individuals fosters a sense of optimism. Despite the cruel treatment and racist attitudes they faced, these men and women never gave up, changing the world with their determination and unique voice. Discovering the triumphs and tragedies of the oppressed allows readers to gain a clearer picture of American history and American cultural identity.

Here to help young readers with this discovery, this series offers a glimpse into the lives and accomplishments of some of the most important and influential African Americans across historical time periods. Titles examine primary source documents and quotes from contemporary thinkers and observers to provide a full and nuanced learning experience for readers. With thoroughly researched text, unique sidebars, and a carefully selected bibliography for further research, this series is an invaluable resource for young scholars. Moreover, it does not shy away from reconciling the brutality of the past with a sense of hopefulness for the future. This series provides critical tools for understanding more about how black history is a vital part of American history.

# SETTING THE SCENE:

**1870**
Hiram R. Revels of Mississippi becomes the first African American to serve in the U.S. Senate; Joseph Rainey of South Carolina is the first African American to serve in the U.S. House of Representatives.

**1937**
William H. Hastie is named to the U.S. District Court of the Virgin Islands to become the first black federal judge.

1836      1870      1872      1937      1965–1967

**1872**
Pinckney Benton Stewart Pinchback of Louisiana becomes the first African American governor.

**1836**
Alexander Twilight is the first African American elected to public office and to a state legislature: the Vermont General Assembly.

**1965–1967**
The Voting Rights Act is passed; President Lyndon B. Johnson makes Robert C. Weaver the first African American member of a president's cabinet; Edward Brooke of Massachusetts is the first African American elected to the U.S. Senate by popular vote; Thurgood Marshall becomes the first African American justice of the U.S. Supreme Court.

# A TIMELINE

**1968–1971**
Shirley Chisholm of New York becomes the first African American woman elected to the U.S. Congress; 13 members of Congress form the Congressional Black Caucus.

**2008–2012**
Barack Obama becomes the first African American Democratic presidential nominee; Obama then becomes the first African American to win a presidential election; Eric Holder becomes the first African American attorney general of the United States; Barack Obama wins his second presidential election.

1968–1971    1989    2001–2005    2008–2012    2017

**2017**
Kamala Harris becomes the second African American woman elected to the U.S. Senate; Ben Carson becomes the secretary of the Department of Housing and Urban Development.

**1989**
Douglas Wilder of Virginia is the first African American elected governor.

**2001–2005**
Colin Powell becomes the first African American U.S. secretary of state; Condoleezza Rice becomes the first African American woman to serve as U.S. secretary of state.

# INTRODUCTION
## FROM ENSLAVEMENT TO THE PRESIDENCY

On July 27, 2004, four years before he was elected to be the first African American president in United States history, Barack Obama delivered the keynote address of the Democratic National Convention in Boston, Massachusetts. In a stirring speech to delegates and a national television audience of tens of millions of viewers, Obama explained that any greatness the United States had achieved was due to the guarantees of equality and liberty its founders made to all citizens in the Declaration of Independence. Obama said,

*We hold these truths to be self-evident, that all men are created equal. That they are endowed by their Creator with certain inalienable rights. That among these are life, liberty and the pursuit of happiness. That is the true genius of America, a faith in the simple dreams of its people, the insistence on small miracles.[1]*

He stated that these powerful promises, issued on July 4, 1776, had enabled him and millions of other African Americans and people of all races to achieve great things despite the color of their skin. Obama claimed, "I stand here knowing that my story is part of the larger American story [and] that, in no other country on earth, is my story even possible."[2]

Shortly after Obama delivered this speech, he won an election to become just the fifth African American senator in U.S. history. He took office in January 2005 as one of thousands of black officials across every level of government. Then, on November 4, 2008, Obama made history when he was elected the first African American president of the United States. He served two terms as the 44th president.

*Obama built his early political career on outstanding service and public speaking skills. He used his experience to win two terms as president.*

Comfort in Virginia, which was the first of 13 colonies that England established in the New World. Aboard that ship were 20 Africans, the first blacks to arrive in the land that would one day become the United States of America. These first Africans had been kidnapped from their homelands and transported to Virginia to be traded for food and supplies. For the next two centuries, hundreds of thousands of captured Africans were brought to the United States. At first, some were treated as indentured servants, while others were enslaved. By the late 1600s, all of these kidnapped Africans were forced to live in slavery.

What Obama did not include in his 2004 speech, however, was that when the Founding Fathers penned those promises, they were only meant for people with white skin. It would take decades before their words would become even partially applicable to black people living in America.

Even though the U.S. slave population would grow to 4 million by 1860, slavery divided the nation from its very beginning. Some northern states opposed slavery and tried to abolish it in the U.S. Constitution in 1787. Southern states, which claimed they needed a source of cheap agricultural labor, defeated the attempt to end slavery before the Constitution was completed. Tensions over slavery between the North and the South increased in

## Blacks Begin Political Participation

On August 20, 1619, the *White Lion,* an English ship, landed at Point

the 18th century when northern states acted to outlaw slavery within their own borders. When Abraham Lincoln was elected president in 1860, the issue exploded into armed conflict. Eleven southern states were so sure Lincoln would end slavery that they seceded from the nation and formed the Confederate States of America. The Confederates began the American Civil War on April 12, 1861, by bombing Fort Sumter, a Union military facility in Charleston, South Carolina.

The North eventually won the Civil War, and that meant the end of slavery across the United States. During the Reconstruction Era that followed the war, the Union army occupied southern states and forced them to adhere to the 13th, 14th, and 15th Amendments, which freed the slaves and gave them the rights the Constitution guaranteed American citizens. Frederick Douglass, a former slave and influential black leader, claimed, "Slavery is not abolished until the black man has the ballot."[3]

Southern blacks soon began voting and trying to elect officials, including many fellow African Americans. During Reconstruction, two black U.S. senators, twenty U.S. representatives, and hundreds of state officials helped govern southern states in which they had once been slaves. When federal officials withdrew their soldiers in 1876 to end Reconstruction, whites began taking the hard-won civil liberties away from blacks, including their right to vote. When southern blacks became unable to vote, the number of southern black officials dwindled almost to nothing.

## An Increase in Elected Black Officials

During Reconstruction, when numerous black officials lived in the South, only a few lived anywhere else in the nation. So few African Americans lived outside the South that they rarely had the voting power to elect other blacks. As black populations steadily increased in northern and western states during the first half of the 20th century, they began electing black officials in these areas.

A large portion of southern African Americans were denied their right to vote—through racist Jim Crow laws and other unconstitutional practices—until the federal government passed the Voting Rights Act of 1965. Over the next 5 years, the number of black elected officials nationally rose until there were 1,469 in 1970. More than a decade into the 21st century, there are more than 10,000 African American elected officials, and that number seems to only be increasing. Since 2000, the world of politics has been increasingly open to

African Americans. President Obama was elected to a second term in 2012, Deval Patrick served as governor of Massachusetts from 2007 until 2015, there are more than 40 black members of the U.S. House of Representatives, and in 2017, there were 3 African American senators (Tim Scott, Kamala Harris, and Cory Booker) serving at the same time.

There are also thousands of black officials who have been appointed to their positions, ranging from school district superintendents to U.S. Attorney General Loretta Lynch, who served from 2015 to 2017. There have been noticeable and significant gains for African American public servants every year since 1965.

## Elections Based on Competence

Although some black elected officials represent districts that are nearly all black, many serve areas with mixed or predominantly nonblack populations. One of them is Ronald Jones, who in 2007, was the first African American to be elected mayor of Garland, Texas, a city where black residents make up less than 20 percent of the population. He served three terms in that position. Ron Kirk, who was elected as the first black mayor of Dallas, Texas, in 1995, said Jones's competence was more responsible for his election than the color of his skin. Kirk said: "[Race] is relevant and it ought to be mentioned. But if you don't have the credentials and experience that people are looking for, it doesn't matter what color you are."[4] People across the United States have learned that African Americans can be politicians just as effectively as whites. That, as well as the fact that blacks can vote without restrictions after having been denied that right for most of the nation's history, is why there are so many black officials today.

# CHAPTER ONE

# A NEW POLITICAL LIFE FOR AFRICAN AMERICANS

Nearly 4 million enslaved African Americans were freed from their bonds when the Civil War ended in 1865. John Mercer Langston knew that African Americans required more than just freedom to be able to lead decent lives. Langston, who was born to a former slave mother and slave-owning father, believed he and other blacks needed the full rights that white citizens had. In a speech in Indianapolis, Indiana, in 1865, Langston said that being able to vote was the most important right blacks needed:

> The colored man is not content when given simple emancipation. That certainly is his due, at once and without condition, but he demands much more than that: he demands absolute legal equality ... There is one thing more, however, he demands; he demands it at the hands of the nation and in all the States. It is the free ... use of the ballot [and the] privilege of saying who shall make our laws, what they shall be, and who shall execute them.[5]

Langston had been elected to public office in two communities in Ohio, even though he himself had never been allowed to vote because of the color of his skin. Langston was one of only a few African Americans elected before the Civil War. All of these pre-war officials were from northern states where slavery was illegal. After the Civil War, the number of blacks elected from southern states began to increase dramatically.

## Equal Rights Under Reconstruction

African American government officials were a rarity until Reconstruction, the historical period that began after the

# THE FIRST BLACK ELECTED OFFICIAL

Alexander Lucius Twilight burst onto the U.S. political scene in the country's first century as an independent nation. Twilight was the first black elected official in U.S. history. On September 6, 1836, he was elected to the Vermont General Assembly. Vermont was the first state to outlaw slavery—it did so in 1777—and was one of the few states that allowed blacks to vote before the Civil War. Twilight was born on September 23, 1795, in Corinth, Vermont, to a free black father, Ichabod, and a white mother, Mary. He attended Middlebury College in Vermont and in 1823, became the first known African American to graduate from a U.S. college. He worked as both a teacher and a minister.

Twilight was instrumental in building a four-story granite building in Brownington known today as the Old Stone House Museum. In the 1830s, Twilight designed and oversaw construction of the building as a student dormitory. This was an amazing accomplishment for the time, and his work inspired the community around him. He occupied his place in Vermont's state legislature until 1857.

*Alexander Lucius Twilight was a groundbreaking black official; his Old Stone House, shown here, was one of his notable accomplishments.*

Civil War and ran until 1877. During this brief but influential period, hundreds of southern blacks were elected or appointed to positions ranging from sheriff to U.S. senator.

During Reconstruction, the federal government re-accepted the 11 defeated Confederate states into the Union, starting with Tennessee in 1866. Alabama, Arkansas, Florida, Georgia, Louisiana, Mississippi, North Carolina, South Carolina, Texas, and Virginia soon followed. The federal government forced southern states to adopt new constitutions that outlawed slavery and gave blacks equal rights with whites, including the right to vote for black men. (Neither white nor black women had the right to vote at this time.) Federal officials also worked with the states to educate former slaves and find them homes and jobs.

Historians believe Reconstruction's most significant consequence was that black officials, many of them former slaves, helped govern the South. One historian wrote, "[Reconstruction] was the first large-scale experiment in interracial democracy that had existed anywhere."[6] This social and political experiment attracted journalists who were curious to see how African Americans functioned as government officials. In 1873, *New York Times* reporter James Pike wrote favorably about black members of the South Carolina legislature:

> *Seven years ago these men were raising corn and cotton under the whip of an overseer. Today they are raising points of order and questions of privilege [in legislative debate]. They can raise one as well as the other. [Their new political power] means liberty. It means the destruction of prison-walls only too real to them. It is the sunshine of their lives.*[7]

## African Americans in State Legislatures

To be readmitted to the Union, southern states had to create new state constitutions that gave more rights to blacks. Hundreds of African Americans helped write these documents, including Francis L. Cardozo, a delegate to the 1868 South Carolina Constitutional Convention. Cardozo was born free in Charleston, South Carolina. He was educated at the University of Glasgow in Scotland, a school he attended because southern states did not commonly allow blacks to attend colleges.

Cardozo proposed a clause for the

# LANGSTON'S VIEWS ON RECONSTRUCTION

In a speech he delivered on May 17, 1874, in Oberlin, Ohio, John Mercer Langston noted how much freedom and Reconstruction helped African Americans:

*Within less than a quarter of a century, within the last fifteen years, the colored American has been raised from the condition of four footed beasts and creeping things to the level of enfranchised manhood. Within this period the slave [rule] of the land has been overthrown, and the nation itself emancipated from its barbarous rule ... For in the death of slavery, and through the change indicated, the colored American has been spoken into the new life of liberty and law [and] the moral atmosphere of the land is no longer that of slavery and hate; as far as the late slave, even, is concerned, it is largely that of freedom and fraternal appreciation.*[1]

1. John Mercer Langston, "Equality Before the Law," Electronic Oberlin Group. www.oberlin.edu/external/EOG/LangstonSpeeches/equality.htm.

*John Mercer Langston was among the most prominent post–Civil War advocates for black rights.*

new constitution that ensured no one could ever take away the new freedom blacks had. Cardozo argued, "As colored men, we have been cheated out of our rights for two centuries. Now that we have the opportunity, I want to fix them in the constitution in such a way that no lawyer, however cunning or astute, can possibly misinterpret the meaning."[8] While ensuring more equal rights was their first priority, African American delegates also proposed free public schools and advocated other progressive ideas.

After the federal government approved the new constitutions, the states held elections in which blacks could vote and run for office. About 2,000 African American officials were elected during the Reconstruction period. African Americans held both local and state offices. Cardozo was the first African American to become the secretary of state, in 1868, and then state treasurer, in 1872, of South Carolina.

In spite of some progress, many whites in America still did not consider blacks their equals. The main reason so many blacks were elected was that more than 100,000 white citizens were barred from voting because they had been Confederate soldiers or served the Confederate government. That dramatically reduced the pool of eligible white voters in southern states. Some former Confederate states even had more eligible black voters than white voters. Still, even some whites also voted for African Americans because they supported the most powerful political party in the South: the Republican Party.

During Reconstruction, hundreds of African Americans served in southern state legislatures. In the decade after the conclusion of the Civil War, many southern state legislatures met with black members for the first time. Some states, where African American candidates were especially appealing, actually had more black representatives than white. James K. Green, a former slave who helped write Alabama's constitution, was a state legislator for eight years. Green said that he and other blacks joyously accepted their new government duties even though it was difficult to do jobs they had never dreamed of doing before: "The tocsin [bell] of freedom sounded and knocked at the door and we walked out like free men and ... shouldered the responsibilities."[9]

Oscar J. Dunn served as Louisiana's first African American lieutenant governor from 1868 until 1871. This also made him the first black statewide elected official anywhere. Dunn was one of a number of African Americans

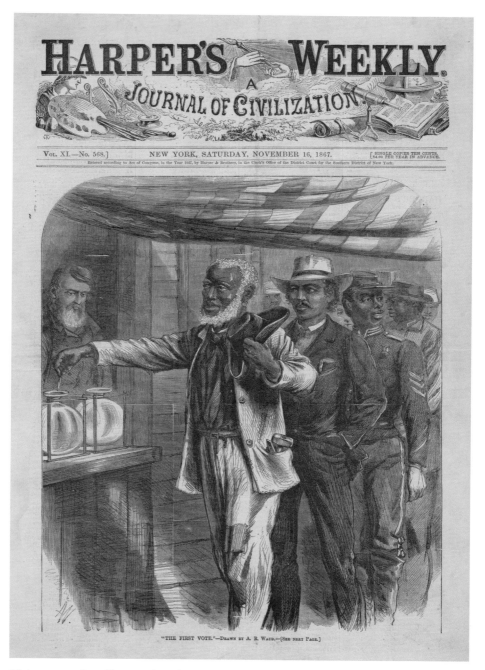

This magazine illustration from 1867 shows African American men casting their first votes.

during Reconstruction who served in state offices, such as treasurer, superintendent of education, and secretary of state.

## P.B.S. Pinchback

Pinckney Benton Stewart Pinchback, the first African American to ever serve as a U.S. governor, was born free in Macon, Georgia, on May 10, 1837. His parents were white plantation owner William Pinchback and Eliza Stewart, a freed slave. When his father died in 1848, his mother moved the family from Mississippi to Ohio to avoid being re-enslaved. By the age of 12, Pinchback was supporting the family.

During the Civil War, Pinchback was a captain in the Union Army. He became active in politics during

Reconstruction, and he helped write Louisiana's new constitution. Pinchback was elected as a Republican to the Louisiana State Senate in 1868 and was named to

*Blanche Kelso Bruce, pictured here, was just the second African American to be elected senator. He served from 1875 until 1881.*

# THE FIRST AFRICAN AMERICANS IN CONGRESS

**Senators**

Hiram Rhodes Revels, 1869–1871 (Mississippi; the first African American senator)

Blanche Kelso Bruce, 1875–1881 (Mississippi; the second African American senator)

**Congressmen**

Joseph Hayne Rainey, 1869–1879 (South Carolina; the first African American representative)

Jefferson Franklin Long, 1869–1871 (Georgia; the second African American representative)

Benjamin Turner, 1871–1873 (Alabama)

Josiah Walls, 1871–1877 (Florida)

John Roy Lynch, 1873–1883 (Mississippi)

John Adams Hyman, 1875–1877 (North Carolina)

Charles Edmund Nash, 1875–1877 (Louisiana)

John Mercer Langston, 1889–1891 (Virginia)

*This drawing shows the first black U.S. senator and congressmen from the 41st and 42nd Congresses.*

replace lieutenant governor Oscar Dunn when he died in 1871.

On December 9, 1872, Louisiana governor Henry Clay Warmoth was impeached and removed from office, and Pinchback became acting governor until his replacement, William P. Kellogg, was sworn in as governor on January 13, 1873. This made Pinchback the first black governor in the United States. Pinchback performed his job well despite threats of violence by whites who did not think an African American should hold such a powerful position. When Pinchback requested a federal ruling about his right to be governor, U.S. attorney general George H. Williams assured him that "You are recognized by the president as the lawful executive of Louisiana."[10] Williams also sent troops to protect Pinchback from racist whites. On the day Kellogg was inaugurated, Pinchback said, "I now have the honor to formally surrender the office of governor, with the hope that... your administration will be as fair toward the class that I especially represent [African Americans] as mine has been to the class that you represent [whites]."[11]

## Rejection of Blacks in Congress

The next day, the State Senate elected Pinchback to the U.S. Senate. (State legislatures chose U.S. senators until 1913, when the U.S. Constitution was changed to let the people of the state choose them.) Pinchback had also been elected to Congress by voters in the election that made Kellogg governor, and Pinchback is the only person ever elected to both houses of Congress at the same time. Pinchback was never able to serve in Congress, however, because his white Democratic opponents falsely claimed he had won through voting irregularities. The Senate and House both ruled against Pinchback and awarded his seats to his opponent.

A few years before this happened to Pinchback, another African American suffered a similar fate. John Willis Menard of Louisiana was the first African American elected to Congress after winning an 1868 election. Not long after winning, Menard became the first black man to speak before the U.S. House of Representatives. However, he was only speaking because he had been unjustly accused of cheating to win his seat. Despite his innocence, the House rejected him and awarded the election to a white representative.

# A LIBERAL CONSTITUTION

Joseph Hayne Rainey helped write the South Carolina constitution. He also served as a U.S. congressman for four terms. During his time as a representative, Rainey gave a speech in which he insisted that he and other African Americans had been fair to whites in creating the constitution and fair in passing new laws:

> I ask the country, I ask white men, I ask Democrats, I ask Republicans whether the Negroes have [taken] improper advantage of the majority they hold in that State by disregarding the interest of the minority? They have not. Our convention which met in 1868, and in which the Negroes were in a large majority, did not pass any [unfair] acts, but adopted a liberal constitution, securing alike equal rights to all citizens, white and black, male and female, as far as possible. Mark you, we did not discriminate, although we had a majority ... You cannot point me to a single act passed by our Legislature, at any time, which had a tendency to reflect upon or oppress any white citizen of South Carolina. You cannot show me one enactment by which the majority in our State have undertaken to crush the white men because [they] are in a minority.[1]

1. Quoted in *Congressional Globe: 42nd Congress, Second Session*. Washington, DC: Government Printing Office, 1872, pp. 1442–1443.

Many white members of Congress, including future president James A. Garfield of Ohio, claimed that it was "too early to admit a Negro to the U.S. Congress."[12]

## The Acceptance of Blacks in Congress

On December 12, 1870, Joseph Hayne Rainey, a Republican from South Carolina, became the first black to be both elected to and accepted by the House as a member of Congress. Overall, 16 African Americans served in the House of Representatives during Reconstruction. Although some had been slaves, most elected politicians had been well educated. Rainey, who was born a slave in 1832 in

*Joseph Hayne Rainey broke ground as a black politician; he paved the way for future African American lawmakers.*

speech to support a bill that aimed to protect southern blacks from the Ku Klux Klan (KKK), a racist group that used violence to deny blacks their rights. His speech helped win passage of the bill.

On February 25, 1870, Hiram Rhodes Revels of Mississippi was sworn in as a U.S. senator. His position would be to fill the seat of Jefferson Davis, who had quit the Senate when he became president of the Confederate States of America. Even though he would only be serving a partial term, senators argued about whether he was worthy of joining the nation's most powerful legislative body. He had not been elected by a popular vote; he was appointed by the Mississippi Legislature to fill Davis's

Georgetown, South Carolina, was reelected to Congress three times and was a member of Congress longer than any other African American during Reconstruction. On April 1, 1871, he delivered a stirring

# A FITTING TRIBUTE

On January 12, 2017, President Barack Obama dedicated the first National Park Service monument to honor Reconstruction. The site, located around Beaufort, South Carolina, was chosen because Beaufort was a Union stronghold during the Civil War. It is also the home of Robert Smalls, a future Civil War hero and powerful politician.

According to historian Eric Foner, honoring these early black politicians is important:

> You were taking your life in your hands by becoming a black political figure. This group of black political leaders suffered more violence, whether it's murder, or arson of their homes or whippings, than any group of political leaders I can think of in American history. Whatever the acrimony of politics right now, you don't have armed men going after members of the legislature and whipping them or shooting them. We're not quite at that level yet. But they were in Reconstruction.[1]

1. Quoted in Zach Young, "Reconstruction Is Finally Getting The Historical Recognition It Deserves," *Huffington Post*. www.huffingtonpost.com/entry/reconstruction-historical-recognition-monument-beaufort-south-carolina_us_58792908e4b09281d0eabb96?atwf02m50t138fr.

position. After he was confirmed, however, he served the remainder of his term successfully.

The first black man to serve a full Senate term was Blanche Kelso Bruce, who was elected in 1874 by the Mississippi senate. Born a slave on March 1, 1841, in Farmville, Virginia, he and his two brothers escaped to Kansas in 1861 and later moved to Mississippi in 1869. He was appointed a tax assessor in his new home and quickly elected sheriff. After Bruce helped Adelbert Ames win election as Mississippi's governor by getting African Americans to vote for him, the State Senate rewarded Bruce by electing him to the U.S. Senate.

Bruce fought racial discrimination against blacks and other groups, including Chinese immigrants and Native Americans. One of his major accomplishments was helping to uncover massive fraud at a federal bank and returning savings to more than 60,000 depositors. He made history on February 14, 1879, when he presided over the Senate in the absence of Vice President William A. Wheeler. The *New York Tribune* newspaper reported, "This is the first time a colored man ever sat in the seat of the Vice-President of the United States. Senator Bruce is universally respected by his fellow senators and is qualified both in manners and character to preside over the deliberations of the most [powerful] body of men in the land."[13]

## Black Politicians' Thoughts on Their Offices

In the late 1800s, African American politicians were empowered by their new positions in government. However, they also realized that they were going to be targets of heavy racial discrimination and countless abuses. Politician Robert Brown Elliot, known as a brilliant speaker, described his first speech in the House of Representatives:

*I shall never forget that day when rising in my place to address the House, I found myself the center of attraction. Everything was still. Those who believed in the natural inferiority of the colored race appeared to feel that the hour had arrived in which they should [celebrate] the failure of the man of "the despised race" whose voice was about to be lifted in that chamber. The [faces] of those who sympathized with our cause seemed to indicate their anxiety for my success, and their heartfelt desire that I might prove equal to the emergency. I cannot picture to you the emotions that then filled my mind.*[14]

For the new generation of black lawmakers, Reconstruction offered both opportunity and immense pressure. The old conservatives of the South wanted them to fail and humiliate themselves. The progressive liberals of the North wanted them to succeed and promote their agenda. During this time period, both sides of the political aisle hoped to use African Americans for their own purposes. The black politicians, however, were mostly concerned with simply doing their jobs. Most historical accounts indicate that black senators and congressmen were well liked and achieved a lot. While nothing in politics is ever perfect, African Americans in power in the 19th century tried to prove they could govern effectively.

Representative Robert Smalls was among these hard-working politicians. Born a slave, he became a Civil War hero when he daringly stole a Confederate ship out of the Charleston harbor and turned it over to the Union navy. Smalls, his wife and children, and several other blacks escaped slavery during this bold move. After the war, Smalls was elected to the South Carolina legislature and then to Congress. He was always concerned with doing his best, and the people he represented believed in him. He served five terms as a congressman.

# CHAPTER TWO
## POLITICAL POWER IS LOST AND REGAINED

African Americans were elected to a variety of political offices during Reconstruction. In spite of these political successes, many whites—in all parts of the United States—still firmly believed that blacks were inherently inferior and not competent to hold office or vote. This racist belief was summed up by South Carolina governor Benjamin Perry, who, shortly after the Civil War ended in 1865, claimed, "This is a white man's government, and intended for white men only."[15]

Blacks were able to gain some political power during Reconstruction because the federal government had stationed thousands of soldiers in the former Confederate states to keep the white officials—and some white citizens—from denying blacks their constitutional rights. However, even the might of the U.S. Army could not change the opinions of many whites or completely stop them from brutal-izing African Americans who dared to exercise those rights.

## The Emergence of Violent Racist Groups

Some southern whites who opposed black equality after the Civil War joined violent groups, such as the KKK, the White League, or the Knights of White Camelia. These racist organizations terrorized African Americans to make them so afraid of whites that they would not dare to exercise their new rights, such as voting, attending school, or owning land. A poorly written note from the KKK to Davie Jeems, a black Republican who had been elected sheriff in Lincoln County, Georgia in 1868 read:

> I am a Ku Klux sent here to look after you and all the rest of the radicals and make you know your place. I have got my eye on you

*every day ... We nail all, radicals up in Boxes and send them away to KKK - there is. 200 000 ded men returned to this country to make you and all the rest of the radicals good Democrats and vote right with the white people.*[16]

Whites knew that the key to blacks winning equality was to have the power to elect officials who would treat them fairly. To prevent this, some whites physically attacked black voters and elected officials. In 1868, a mob in Camilla, Georgia, killed a number of African Americans at a Republican rally. On April 13, 1873, a large group of whites murdered more than 100 African Americans in Colfax, Louisiana, in a dispute over the November 1872 gubernatorial election. When the rightfully elected African American officials tried to take their positions, whites formed a mob

*This illustration from 1872 shows some of the dangers African Americans faced from the Ku Klux Klan.*

and resorted to violence. The mob then went on a rampage throughout Colfax, destroying homes and businesses and killing African Americans in Reconstruction's bloodiest race riot.

During Reconstruction, whites threatened or assaulted dozens of black officials. Abram Colby, a Georgia state congressman, was beaten on October 29, 1869, by KKK members who were furious that he was planning to run in the next election. The attackers beat him nearly to death for refusing to back down, and he lived with difficult medical issues for the rest of his life. Andrew J. Flowers was whipped after being elected justice of the peace in Tennessee. He said Klan members told him they did it "because I had the impudence to run against a white man for office, and beat him."[17] Both survived the beatings, but more than 30 African American officials died in similar attacks. Despite such violence, hundreds of thousands of black voters in this period were not intimidated and elected about 2,000 African Americans into office.

## A Political Deal Ends Reconstruction

White Republicans, such as Senator Charles Sumner of Massachusetts, believed blacks deserved equal rights, especially the power to vote. "This is the Great Guarantee," Sumner said of voting rights, "without which all other guarantees will fail."[18] Although the Republicans had used their political power to impose Reconstruction on the South to help blacks, they also had a political motive for creating Reconstruction: They wanted to establish themselves as the dominant party over the Democrats.

The Democratic Party had always been powerful in the South because of its previous support of slavery. When African Americans began voting, they nearly always voted Republican because that party had ended slavery (Abraham Lincoln was a Republican.) and given them their new rights. Black voters immediately strengthened the Republican Party in southern states. In addition, hundreds of thousands of former Confederate whites, who were largely Democrats, were not allowed to vote for several years as punishment for waging the Civil War. Those two factors helped the Republican Party win southern states so it could elect Republican Ulysses Grant president in 1868 and again in 1872.

Republican political power began to fade in the mid-1870s as new western states began voting for Democrats. The Democrats also grew stronger in southern states when huge numbers of former Confederate soldiers and

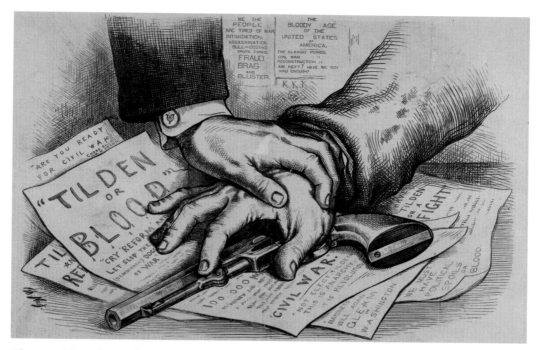

*Thomas Nast drew this political cartoon in response to the Compromise of 1877. It symbolized the tension that still existed between Democrats and Republicans.*

officials became eligible to vote again. By 1876, only Florida, Louisiana, and South Carolina still had Republican-controlled governments.

This situation created a political crisis in the 1876 presidential election between Democrat Samuel Tilden and Republican Rutherford B. Hayes. When both parties claimed victory in Florida, Louisiana, and South Carolina, a new Electoral Commission—which included both Democrats and Republicans—was created by the Congress. Eventually, this commission awarded the states to Hayes, giving him 185 electoral votes to

Tilden's 184. The decision was based on a political deal between the two parties and not actual popular vote numbers. It became known as the Compromise of 1877. The Republicans wanted to retain the presidency so much that they offered to give the votes to Hayes so he could become president. In return, Hayes would end Reconstruction, pull federal troops out of southern states, and allow whites to govern southern states without interference from the federal government. The two parties agreed to the deal, and Hayes was sworn in as president on March 2, 1877.

# LITERACY TESTS

Literacy tests were one of the most visible of the Jim Crow laws that erupted in the South after Reconstruction. These tests were used to prevent black men,

and sometimes poor white men, from voting. (Women were not allowed to vote at all at this time.) There were no strict rules or regulations for administering literacy tests. The format, style, questions, and acceptable answers were usually left up to the white officials who were registering voters. They could vary the number or difficulty of the questions at will. These tests were universally negative for African Americans. Thousands of hopeful voters were turned away on Election Day because of these racist tests.

*This political cartoon shows Uncle Sam—a symbol of America—creating a literacy test to keep blacks from voting.*

Hayes defended the political compromise, saying he was sure that "absolute justice and fair play to the negro [was possible] by trusting the honorable and influential southern whites."[19] Most other observers, however, believed that this compromise was going to have disastrous results for African American freedom in southern politics—and they were right.

## Changes to Southern Constitutions

In South Carolina, Democratic governor Wade Hampton ordered dozens of his state's black officials to quit. Among these were the state's attorney general, Robert Brown Elliott, who had worked closely with Hampton in the past. Though Elliott tried to fight to preserve his position, the state supreme court sided with Hampton. The court's white justices, who knew Elliott had been legally elected, still allowed Hampton to remove him. They also did not want African Americans serving as officials. The federal government refused to do anything to stop such unjust dismissals.

When Reconstruction ended in 1877, Robert Toombs of Georgia, a former U.S. senator and Confederate general said, "Give us a convention, and I will fix it so that [white] people shall rule and the Negro shall never be heard from."[20] During the next 20 years, southern states rewrote or revised their constitutions and passed new laws designed to deny African Americans the right to vote.

Toombs helped draft a new Georgia constitution that included a poll tax people had to pay before they could vote. Many African Americans at the time were so poor they could not afford it. Other measures to reduce black voters included literacy tests, which many blacks could not pass because they had never gone to school, and party primary elections open only to white voters.

The federal government did not stop southern states from denying blacks those rights, even though the 14th Amendment made African Americans full citizens and the 15th Amendment prohibited denying any citizen the right to vote, regardless of race, color, or previous condition of enslavement. Congress refused to do anything for nearly a century because it largely did not care about the suffering of African Americans living in racist states.

Whites continued to attack individual blacks who dared to vote and also conducted large-scale episodes of racial violence. One incident occurred in Wilmington, North Carolina, on November 10, 1898, when a mob of 500 whites led by Alfred Moore Waddell took control of the city and forced black and white Republican officials to resign. Even though at least 14 African Americans were killed in the brutal takeover of Wilmington's government, neither state nor federal officials punished anyone. According to J. Allen Kirk, a black minister who witnessed the riot, "The woods were filled with colored people. The streets

# LANGSTON CITY, OKLAHOMA

In 1890, Edward P. McCabe and William L. Eagleson, both prominent black citizens, joined with Charles W. Robbins, a white real estate dealer, to establish the African American community of Langston City in the Oklahoma Territory. They chose the name to honor John Mercer Langston, a newly elected congressman. African Americans from nearby Kansas and southern states flocked to the new city. Within a year, the city had a population of about 600, with more settlers living nearby. McCabe started a newspaper, *The Langston City Herald.* Others started schools, businesses, churches, and banks. In 1897, the Colored Agricultural and Normal School of Oklahoma (now Langston University) was founded.

Although the town never grew as large as the founders expected, it did survive; Langston City is a town in Oklahoma. In 2016, the population was about 1,457, with about 93 percent being black. Langston University continues to flourish and provide higher education to people of all races.

*This photograph shows one of the first classes at Langston's school.*

were dotted with their dead bodies."[21] The violent riot in Wilmington proved African Americans all across the country were still in danger every day.

By 1900, the cumulative effect of discriminatory state laws, white intimidation, and federal indifference reduced the number of black voters to only a fraction of eligible southern blacks; black officeholders then became a rarity in the South for nearly a century.

## Black Representation in Congress

The small number of African American voters also affected black representation in Congress. U.S. representative George Henry White, the last former slave to serve in Congress, was elected in 1896 and 1898 from his native North Carolina. The state had a sizable number of black voters until 1900, when its legislature passed literacy and poll tax laws that significantly restricted the number of African American voters.

As a result, White was defeated when he ran for reelection in 1900. By 1910, black voting in North Carolina had been almost entirely eliminated. Another black congressman would not be elected until 1928, when Oscar Stanton De Priest of Illinois became the first African American elected to Congress from a northern state. De Priest's election symbolized a significant shift in the history of black elected officials.

The Reconstruction period was the first time large numbers of blacks held office, but that occurred only in the South because so few African Americans lived in other areas. This situation started changing after Reconstruction when blacks began leaving the South. They moved to northern and western states because southern whites denied them their rights and employed violence to keep them submissive. Lynch mobs, commonly formed by radical whites and KKK members, would round up and hang African Americans who spoke out against white supremacy. About 95 percent of the 3,446 black people lynched in the United States between 1882 and 1968 were murdered in the South.

The first wave of African Americans to move from the South were called Exodusters. This name was taken from Exodus, which was the biblical account of how the Jewish people fled slavery in Egypt. In 1879 and 1880, tens of thousands of blacks left Mississippi, Louisiana, and other southern states for Kansas, which had opposed slavery before the Civil War. Edward P. McCabe, who was born a free black in Troy, New York, also moved to Kansas so he could help African Americans start new towns. McCabe became a leading Republican Party official and in 1882, was elected state auditor. In 1884, he was reelected to that position, but in the 1886 election, racism prevented his victory. A few years later, McCabe joined thousands of blacks who migrated to the Oklahoma Territory, an area he claimed could be a fresh start for African Americans: "Here the negro can rest from mob law, here he can be secure from every ill of the southern policies."[22] In 1890, McCabe was instrumental in the founding of Langston City, which was a black community. African Americans were able to create communities in such unpopulated western areas because no white settlers were there to bother them.

Between 1916 and 1970, in what is now known as the Great Migration, about 6 million African Americans left the South for large northern and western cities, including New York City; Chicago, Illinois; Pittsburgh, Pennsylvania; and Cleveland, Ohio. They moved in search of better jobs and to escape the intense segregation and discrimination of the South. The pace of this historic migration peaked during World War I, when an estimated 450,000 blacks headed north. This population shift enabled the election of black officials. Oscar De Priest, for example, was elected to the Cook County, Illinois, board of commissioners in 1904. As Chicago's black population grew in size and political strength, De Priest was elected to more powerful positions. He became the city's first black alderman in 1915 and then a congressman. This pattern of black migration and political growth repeated itself in many other cities.

African American officials in the South in the first half of the 20th century were extremely rare because whites did not let blacks vote. One notable exception was Charles W. Anderson, who in 1935, won a seat in the Kentucky General Assembly to become the first southern black state legislator since Reconstruction. Racial discrimination was still dominant across every southern state, however, and this unjust situation did not change until blacks began fighting for their civil rights in the 1950s.

## A New Era

The civil rights struggle that finally ended such discrimination began in 1956, when African Americans in Montgomery, Alabama, led by Martin Luther King Jr., began a protest that erased a law that forced blacks to sit in the rear of buses and give up their seats to whites. That small but important victory soon ignited other protests in the South to allow blacks to eat in restaurants, shop in stores, and stay in hotels that were traditionally reserved for whites. In the 1960s, this historic battle began to focus on the biggest issue of all: the right to vote.

The largest civil rights rally of this turbulent era occurred on August 28, 1963, in Washington, D.C. This day is remembered because of a powerful speech delivered by King,

# PRESIDENT JOHNSON SIGNS THE VOTING RIGHTS ACT OF 1965

On August 6, 1965, President Lyndon B. Johnson signed the Voting Rights Act. He said in part,

*Millions of Americans are denied the right to vote because of their color. This law will ensure them the right to vote. The wrong is one which no American, in his heart, can justify. The right is one which no American, true to our principles, can deny ... So, let me now say to every Negro in this country: You must register. You must vote. You must learn, so your choice advances your interest and the interest of our beloved Nation. Your future, and your children's future, depend upon it, and I don't believe that you are going to let them down ... If you do this, then you will find, as others have found before you, that the vote is the most powerful instrument ever devised by man for breaking down injustice and destroying the terrible walls which imprison men because they are different from other men.*[1]

1. Lyndon Baines Johnson, "President Johnson Speech at Voting Rights Act Passage," Communities Against Hate. www.civilrights.org/voting-rights/vra/johnson-speech.html.

who told 250,000 people he had a dream that whites and blacks would one day live in harmony. King said a key element to realizing that dream was the right of blacks to vote: "We can never be satisfied as long as a Negro in Mississippi cannot vote and a Negro in New York believes he has nothing for which to vote. No, no, we are not satisfied, and we will not be satisfied until justice rolls down like waters and righteousness like a mighty stream."[23]

Whites brutally beat blacks who tried to register to vote and murdered blacks and whites who led drives to register black voters. This racial hatred was displayed in Selma, Alabama, on March 7, 1965, a day that became known as "Bloody Sunday." When 600 marchers, mostly black but with some white supporters, organized a peaceful march from Selma to Montgomery for the

*Though the civil rights movement created great changes to the United States, racist whites often responded violently to demonstrations by African American activists.*

right to vote, state troopers and county sheriff's deputies stopped them from crossing the Edmund Pettus Bridge so they could not continue their protest. Law enforcement officials fired tear gas at protesters and beat them with whips and clubs until they retreated. Reports estimate that 50 people were put in the hospital due to wounds sustained at the hands of violent policemen. The entire event was televised, and the news reports shocked both the nation and the world.

On March 9, King, who by 1965, was the most prominent African American activist in the world, organized and led another peaceful march from Selma to Montgomery. Rather than see his followers beaten and attacked again, however, he turned the march around when Alabama authorities blocked their path once more.

On March 15, Democratic President Lyndon B. Johnson addressed Congress. Declaring that he believed every American, regardless of race, should have their right to vote protected, Johnson proposed the Voting Rights Act of 1965. The law reaffirmed the absolute right of blacks to vote and, more importantly, provided federal enforcement to ensure they could exercise that right. Attempts by southern congressmen to kill the bill delayed its passage, but Johnson finally signed it into law on August 6, 1965.

# CHAPTER THREE
# AFRICAN AMERICANS
# IN LOCAL GOVERNMENT

Victories achieved during the civil rights movement of the 1960s helped bring about national changes. The United States had 300 black elected officials in 1964 and nearly 1,500 by 1970. Historians have concluded that the decade of the 1960s saw the greatest leap forward in political equality for African Americans to date. From being shut out from the polls to holding major elected offices, it was a landmark decade for equality in America.

By the 21st century, the number of black elected mayors, councilmembers, and other officials in the United States has grown to more than 10,000. There are hundreds of African Americans in major positions of power, including congressmen, senators, and even the nation's first black president, Barack Obama.

Black politicians at local levels have achieved widespread success as well. Across many cities, there are African Americans occupying elected government positions.

## Initial Victories in the South

On May 6, 1969, Howard Lee was elected mayor in Chapel Hill, North Carolina. Lee won by 400 votes out of a record 4,734 cast by voters in a community that was almost entirely made up of whites. After his narrow victory, Lee admitted he worried about people "both black and white, who constantly wonder whether a black man is really capable of handling the reins of municipal government."[24] However, Lee did such a good job serving as Chapel Hill's mayor that he was overwhelmingly elected to serve an additional two terms after his first.

Charles Evers became Mississippi's first black elected official in nearly a century when, on May 13, 1969, he defeated R.J. "Turnip Green" Allen in the Fayette, Mississippi, mayoral election. Fayette was a small, racially mixed town of around 2,000 people at the time. His election was significant not just because he broke down a racial barrier in highly conservative Mississippi, but also because his brother, Medgar Evers, had been shot to death on June 12, 1963, by a white supremacist in Jackson, Mississippi, for leading the fight for black rights in that state.

The first black mayor of a southern city with 50,000 or more residents was Clarence Lightner of Raleigh, North Carolina. He was elected in 1973, after serving for six years on the city council. His victory was especially significant because he not only won a mayoral campaign in a major metropolitan area, he also won in a city that was historically conservative and overwhelmingly white.

Many other African Americans have since headed southern cities. In 1977, Ernest Morial was elected mayor of New Orleans, Louisiana.

(His son Marc Morial became the city's mayor in 1994.) In 1991, Willie Herenton was elected mayor of Memphis, Tennessee, and served for a total of five terms. In 2001, Shirley Franklin's election as mayor of Atlanta made her the first African American

*This photo shows Ernest Morial, who was the first black mayor of New Orleans, a major southern city.*

# PERKINS WINS IN SELMA

As a 12-year-old, James Perkins Jr. witnessed Bloody Sunday in Selma, and what he saw shocked him: "I ran out the back door [of the family home] and down to Brown Chapel church, where the marchers were reconvening. I saw them, tear gas in their eyes, beaten up."[1] Selma's mayor, Joe Smitherman, had done nothing to stop the brutal attacks because blacks could not vote him out of office. Smitherman had actually been wildly popular with Selma's residents, and he served as mayor for more than 30 years. Perkins was the candidate who finally beat Smitherman on September 12, 2000. He was the first African American to serve as Selma's mayor. His victory marked a major turning point for historically racially unequal cities. Historian Frank Sikora said, "Blacks have won offices across the South, but none is as important a symbol as this one."[2] Perkins's victory was significant because blacks across the county still considered Selma a symbol of the racism that had denied them their rights for so long.

1. Quoted in Florestine Purnell, "Bridge Builder," *People*, November 6, 2000. people.com/archive/bridge-builder-vol-54-no-19/.

2. Quoted in Purnell, "Bridge Builder."

*James Perkins Jr. won an important battle for African American equality when he was elected Selma's mayor in 2000.*

woman to serve as a mayor and the first female mayor of Atlanta. That same year, Yvonne Brown broke racial and political barriers as the first African American female Republican mayor of Mississippi when she won in Tchula. As this century goes onward, cities across the country are electing their first African American leaders, and many of these politicians are women.

## Black Mayors in Northern Cities

Since racism was not as strong in the northern and western states, the nation's first black mayors came to power in cities in those areas. Robert C. Henry became the nation's first African American mayor in 1966 when he took office in Springfield, Illinois. Though this was an incredible accomplishment, Henry's term as mayor is commonly overshadowed by Carl B. Stokes, who won election in Cleveland, just six months later in 1967.

Stokes's victory in Cleveland made him the first black mayor of a city with a large population. He knew this was a political milestone. He was the grandson of a slave, and he beat Seth Taft, grandson of former U.S. president William Howard Taft. His election signaled a new era of African American political power. Though it had taken hundreds of years, African Americans finally found themselves in positions where they could be seen as equals. Within a decade of these early victories, hundreds of African American mayors were elected, and by 1990, black mayors had headed three of the country's largest cities: Thomas Bradley in Los Angeles, California (1973), Harold Washington in Chicago (1983), and David Dinkins in New York City (1990).

The struggle of southern blacks to vote ignited a new passion for political activity in African Americans around the nation. That new attitude was coupled with the growth of black populations in inner-city areas, which was caused by poverty, segregated housing patterns, and racial discrimination. These impoverished but passionate citizens wanted to elect someone who could help improve their lives. Often, they turned to African American politicians.

Black mayors worked to improve the lives of African Americans. They hired more blacks for city jobs. They curbed discriminatory treatment of blacks by local police and provided blacks with better access to housing, social services, and schools. Just as important, they gave black residents new hope for the future. When Bradley ran unsuccessfully for Los Angeles mayor in 1969, he explained one reason why he wanted the job: "I want to provide a sense of hope for our young people. I want them to be able to look at city hall and know that the system can work ... I want them to know that we can reshape the structure [of government]."[25]

Though many prejudicial white voters believed that an African American mayor would only care about issues affecting black people, most black mayors also did a lot to help white citizens. This was not just the right thing to do, it also helped them stay in power. After all, in most cities, African Americans were the minority. White votes were important, and after seeing how well black mayors did, many whites were willing to vote for them.

## An Increase in Black Mayors

In 1970, there were 81 black mayors in the United States. That number grew to 480 in 2001, including more than 30 who served cities with populations greater than 50,000. In 2017, there were more than 500 African American mayors serving more than 48 million constituents.

Many African American politicians have been elected mayors of cities with few black residents, including Norman Rice in Seattle, Washington, in 1989; Wellington E. Webb in Denver, Colorado, in 1991; and James C. Hayes in Fairbanks, Alaska,

in 1994. Originally from Sacramento, California, Hayes once said, "In Fairbanks, people tend to accept you as you are. They just want to hear your platform and hear what you believe in, and then see you go out and work really hard."[26] Though not all American cities were equally accepting of black politicians, most African American leaders believed that they could win election and reelection by working their hardest.

Webb was mayor of Denver from 1991 to 2003. Webb once said, "Previously, we were not given the chance to run, but we have shown that whether a city is in a predominantly black or white area, we can do a good job."[27] During his time as mayor, Webb received praise for improving the city's economy by fostering commercial and residential redevelopment and reclaiming park land for citizens to enjoy along the South Platte River.

Ron Kirk was elected mayor of Dallas, Texas, on May 6, 1995, because he convinced white voters he could help the city improve economically as well as bring more racial harmony to the city, which had large black and Hispanic populations. "It doesn't matter whether your ancestors came over on the Mayflower or a slave ship. We're all in the same boat now,"[28] Kirk said in his victory speech. In two terms, Kirk

# MAYORS OF WASHINGTON, D.C.

Since 1975, Washington, D.C., has had seven mayors. All have been Democrats, and all have been African American. Walter Washington served from 1975 until 1979. He was known for making direct contact with his constituents. Marion Barry beat him in 1979 and served until 1991 and again from 1995 to 1999. Also known for his work as a civil rights activist, Barry died in 2014. Sharon Pratt, a lifelong resident of the city and former treasurer for the Democratic National Convention, was the city's first African American woman mayor. She served her term from 1991 to 1995. Anthony Williams was mayor from 1999 until 2007. One of his main focuses was economic development. He was succeeded by Adrian Fenty, followed by Vincent Gray, each of whom served for one term. Muriel Bowser began her term on January 2, 2015. She has worked to increase jobs and improve economic stability in the city.

helped create the Trinity River Corridor Project, a $246 million plan for parks and highways in the Trinity River flood plain, and advocated for the construction of the American Airlines Center, which opened in 2002 and hosts the Dallas Mavericks of the National Basketball Association (NBA) and the Dallas Stars of the National Hockey League (NHL). Both projects were

*Walter Washington (far left), Marion Barry (left), Sharon Pratt (top left), Anthony Williams (top right), Adrian Fenty (bottom left), and Vincent Gray (bottom right) all proved to be effective mayors. Some focused on education or employment, while others tried to improve housing or balance the budget, but they all contributed to a rich history of African American political leadership.*

considered economically beneficial for his community.

The year 2015 was a successful one for the election of black mayors in the state of Georgia. Al Thurman became the first black mayor of Powder Springs, defeating his white opponent. Only a few miles away, in Douglasville, Rochelle Robinson became both the first woman and the first African American to hold

# THE FIRST BLACK WOMEN MAYORS

In recent years, African American women have been elected mayors of both large and small cities. Among the most prominent is Muriel Bowser of Washington, D.C., who was elected in 2014. Even before her time in office, however, black women had a rich tradition of political success at a local level. Beginning in 1973, when Lelia Foley was elected mayor in Taft, Oklahoma, and Doris A. Davis was elected mayor in Compton, California, women have shattered racial and gender barriers all across the United States. In 2001, Shirley Franklin was elected mayor of Atlanta, Georgia, becoming the first female African American to head a major city. Other women who served as mayor include: Yvonne Brown (Tchula, Mississippi, 2001); Rhine McLin (Dayton, Ohio, 2002); Yvonne Johnson (Greensboro, North Carolina, 2007); Vivian Pounder (Damascus, Georgia, 2009); Karen Freeman-Wilson (Gary, Indiana, 2012); Ollie Tyler (Shreveport, Louisiana, 2014); and Mary Moore (Pearsall, Texas, 2015 ).

Many women have achieved two firsts by being elected: the first African American and the first woman mayor. Among them are: Ludmya "Mia" Love (Saratoga Springs, Utah, 2009); Acquanetta Warren (Fontana, California, 2010); Louvenia Diane Lumpkin (Orrville, Alabama, 2012); and JoAnn Bennett Grimsley (Midland City, Alabama, 2016).

*Muriel Bowser, shown here, was the second female African American mayor in Washington, D.C., a city with a long history of diverse political elections.*

the office. In Fayetteville, Ed Johnson won 54 percent of the votes in a city that is only one-third African American. Johnson had previously been that city's first black councilmember. The president of one branch of the National Association for the Advancement of Colored People (NAACP) said, "He's a person who can attract support from those who historically differ from African American views. He's a bridge-builder."[29]

On the West Coast, Michael Tubbs became the first African American mayor of his hometown of Stockton, California, in 2016. At age 26, he is also the youngest mayor in Stockton history. Prior to taking office, Tubbs had served as a councilman for four years.

Earlier, in Newark, New Jersey, 29-year-old Democrat Cory Booker also started his political career as a city councilmember, serving from 1998 until 2002. He was elected mayor in 2006 and served two terms. In 2013, he was elected to the U.S. Senate.

## Creating Change on Local Levels

From Georgia to California, African

---

# THE NEW SOUTHERN MIGRATION

In the 1970s, African Americans began moving back to southern states. By 2010, almost 1 million blacks had moved back to both urban and suburban areas in the South, especially in Georgia, North Carolina, Texas, and Florida. At the same time, the black populations of New York, Illinois, Michigan, and California shrank considerably. Some historians have cited race riots and job losses in the northern cities as two of the main reasons for the change.

However, many are chasing the economic security that caused their families to flee the South years ago. One historian noted, "It's an economic pull, plus those traditions and that cultural tie. College-graduate blacks, they can pretty much move anywhere they want to when there's a good economy, and they choose to move to Southern states."[1]

1. Quoted in Greg Toppo and Paul Overberg, "After Nearly 100 Years, Great Migration Begins Reversal," *USA Today*. www.usatoday.com/story/news/nation/2015/02/02/census-great-migration-reversal/21818127/.

Americans elected to city councils and county boards have initiated programs and passed laws to help their fellow citizens. Velvalea "Vel" Phillips was one of the earliest African American city councilors. In 1956, she became the first woman and first African American elected to the city council in Milwaukee, Wisconsin. After the council repeatedly rejected legislation she introduced to end housing discrimination, she joined nightly protest marches and was even arrested. In 1968, the council finally approved the Fair Housing Law Phillips had first proposed six years earlier. She was just one of many black politicians who wanted to reduce and remove the discrimination that was still existent across many areas of daily life.

Many African Americans fought to desegregate schools by winning seats on school boards across the nation. In 1965, Rachel Bassette Noel was the first African American elected to the Denver Public Schools Board of Education, as well as the first black woman elected to any public office in Colorado. On April 25, 1968, she introduced the Noel Resolution, which sought to guarantee equal educational opportunity for all children by integrating Denver schools. The board passed the resolution in February 1970. Noel later said, "I ran for the board of education so [it] would have a black voice and integrate the schools ... I wanted people to know that because we were black we didn't have less worth or value. We were not to be judged by the color of our skins."[30]

## From Cities to States

Though there were many African American city councilors, mayors, and even federal representatives to be found in the 20th century, there were few statewide officials. For many whites, who stuck closely to traditions, the important task of ruling an entire state was too critical to hand over to a black politician. Knowing that they would most likely meet failure, many African Americans did not even bother to run for governorships. Most blacks saw the widespread election of African American local leaders and were generally happy with what had been accomplished. It was nearly the 21st century before an African American finally won a gubernatorial race.

# CHAPTER FOUR

# BLACK POLITICIANS IN STATES AND TERRITORIES

The end of Reconstruction also marked the end of black governorships for 100 years. Then, on November 8, 1989, Democratic candidate Douglas Wilder shattered an important racial barrier when he was elected governor of Virginia. The odds were long for Wilder's election, as more than 75 percent of the voters in Virginia were white; without them, Wilder's success could not be guaranteed.

Wilder prevailed, and at his inauguration on January 13, 1990, he referenced another famous Virginian, Thomas Jefferson, who was a Founding Father and author of the Declaration of Independence, when he said, "We mark today not the victory of party or the accomplishments of an individual but the triumph of an idea ... The idea that all men are created equal."[31] It was a deeply symbolic victory; Virginia, the first state to import slaves and the capital of the Confederacy during the Civil War, was the first state to elect a black governor.

Wilder's success was followed by Deval Patrick when, in 2006, the Democrat was elected governor of Massachusetts. Patrick kept the governorship until 2015. Just two years after Patrick's victory, another Democrat, David Paterson, began serving as governor of New York.

The U.S. Virgin Islands, an organized unincorporated island territory of the United States, have a history of African American leadership. In 1946, President Harry Truman named William Hastie governor of the islands. Since then, the U.S. Virgin Islands have had many black governors.

Despite the recent progress in national politics, African American governors are still a relative

*Douglas Wilder broke new ground when he won the
1989 gubernatorial election in Virginia. His success led
to a string of African American governorships across
the country.*

## The Early 20th Century

In addition to governorships, there were few positions available for African Americans in most statewide bodies in general. The rare pioneering officials were often subjected to racism even after they were elected. In 1957, Cecil Partee of Chicago was elected to the Illinois state legislature. Due to segregation, he said, "When I first got there ... it was impossible for a black legislator to live in one of the hotels."[32] Partee later served in the Illinois Senate and was the first black senate president in that state.

In 1962, a breakthrough occurred when Edward W. Brooke was elected attorney general in Massachusetts and Gerald A. Lamb became treasurer in Connecticut. Despite their historic victories, the entire nation

rarity. Since Patrick left office in 2015, Kenneth Mapp, governor of the U.S. Virgin Islands, was the only African American serving as governor of any kind as of 2017.

still had few African American state officials before Congress passed the Voting Rights Acts of 1965. Once blacks were free to vote, the number of officials grew quickly; before the end of the 20th century, hundreds of African Americans held high state offices. As the 21st century progresses, there are increasingly higher numbers of black officials in state governments.

## Shattering a Racial Barrier

One of the first black politicians to break through statewide racial barriers was Wilder, who achieved several political firsts. In 1969, he was the first African American elected to the Virginia senate since Reconstruction. In his first senate speech in February 1970, Wilder asked Virginia to stop using "Carry Me Back to Old Virginny" as its state song because of offensive lyrics that glorified slavery and referred to blacks as "darkies." The state kept the song, but Wilder became popular with fellow African Americans for advocating civil rights causes. He also quickly won white supporters by championing economically conservative policies to keep taxes low and working to strengthen the state's financial stability.

Wilder became so popular that, in 1985, he was elected lieutenant governor. This made him the first African American to hold statewide executive office in the South since Reconstruction. Wilder said he hoped his election victory would show other African Americans that they could accomplish great things despite lingering racism. "You can't give up, you can't believe that your origin, your birth status must be a detraction,"[33] he said.

Four years later, Wilder was elected governor when he narrowly defeated white Republican J. Marshall Coleman. Wilder won by 6,741 votes, less than 1 percent, in the tightest gubernatorial race in the state's history. Wilder's victory shattered a racial barrier in politics that some whites thought would never be broken. He had proven, once and for all, that an African American could become an American governor in the post–Civil War world.

After Wilder won, he insisted that his victory in a state with a black population under 20 percent showed that voters did not care about race. He firmly maintained that his race was not relevant: "It is not and it was not a factor in the results because I was elected."[34] Election returns, however, showed that it did matter

# A SUCCESS FOR ALL RACES

Douglas Wilder was the grandson of slaves; however, his parents provided a stable home for their eight children. Wilder graduated in 1951 from Virginia Union University, which was then a black college in Richmond, Virginia. As an army solider during the Korean War, he was awarded a Bronze Star for bravery. In 1959, Wilder received his law degree from Howard University in Washington, D.C.; at that time, African Americans were not allowed to go to law school in Virginia. Wilder then opened a law practice in his hometown of Richmond. He soon became involved in politics, and, in 1985, he became Virginia's first black lieutenant governor. Not long after he was sworn in, the *Washington Post* reported about his victory:

> *The 54-year-old Richmond lawyer and legislator appears to be neither bitter about the past nor boastful of the future ... he doesn't shy away from pointing out his support of issues important to blacks. On equal housing, food stamps ... and black colleges [he said], "I was there." [However,] Wilder says he resisted the temptation to "restrict my sphere of influence to color."*[1]

1. Quoted in Donald P. Baker, "Roots of Wilder Victory," *Washington Post*, November 7, 1985. www.washingtonpost.com/archive/politics/1985/11/07/roots-of-wilder-victory/ce3ac6d6-39e8-4f84-a188-4ed767c6d4ef/?utm_term=.46c77195da72.

to some Virginians—in some heavily white districts, Wilder did not get as many votes as other Democratic candidates. His election was also by an extremely narrow margin, which meant that many people who did not support Wilder were ready to criticize whatever he did as governor, even if it was beneficial to the citizens of Virginia.

## Meeting Challenges

Wilder met his first challenge as governor by erasing a $2.2 billion state budget deficit. He won praise by freezing state hiring and making deep, reasonable cuts in spending. Even while minding the budget, he appointed a record number of minorities and women to state jobs. He also initiated a law to slow and regulate the sale of handguns.

Wilder received some criticism for using the prestige of his office to attempt to win the Democratic nomination for president. When Wilder's candidacy was unable to gain traction, he dropped out of the race in January 1992 to concentrate on governing Virginia. Wilder admitted then that "Balancing the [challenges] of running a state government and conducting a national campaign have not been easy."[35] In his final two years in office, Wilder had mixed success as governor, mainly because Virginia continued to struggle financially due to a national economic recession. Most people believed Wilder could possibly have won reelection, but Virginia governors are not allowed to serve two consecutive terms. In his last appearance as governor, in January 1994, Wilder said he hoped other African Americans would be inspired by his political achievement.

## Governor Deval Patrick

Though the nation was without a black governor from 1994 until 2006, Wilder's achievement had broken new ground for African Americans. In 2006, Deval Patrick was elected governor of Massachusetts. Patrick was born on July 31, 1956, and lived in a poor area of Chicago. His hard work as a student eventually gained him a scholarship to the prestigious Milton Academy in Massachusetts. He then graduated from Harvard University and continued on to Harvard Law School.

Patrick made headlines as head of the U.S. Justice Department's civil rights division from 1994 to 1997; after that, he worked as a federal judge and in the private sector for large companies. In 2005, he announced his candidacy for the governorship of Massachusetts. During his campaign, both blacks and whites were drawn to Patrick because of his charismatic personality and their belief that his corporate and government experience would make him a good governor. Patrick also enjoyed success because of his history of civil rights activism. In a 1996 article, he wrote, "The notion of equality is never even mentioned in public discourse ... as if avoiding the subject avoids the problem ... Indeed, race relations is the only major social ill today that we are seriously considering curing by denial."[36]

A Democrat, Patrick achieved a landslide victory in a predominately white state. His election not only made him just the third African American governor in U.S. history, Patrick was so popular that he persuaded hundreds of thousands

*Deval Patrick used his impressive credentials as a lawyer and judge to win election as governor of Massachusetts. He was renowned for his speaking skills.*

fund affordable housing, implemented health care reform, and won a Race to the Top federal education grant worth $250 million. Patrick also enforced new policies to respect the rights of minority populations. He served as governor until 2015.

## Governor David Paterson

David Paterson had many years of government service before he became New York's first, and the nation's fourth, black governor in 2008. In addition to overcoming racial prejudices, Paterson is legally blind. Paterson was born in 1954 and is a lifelong resident of the state of New York. After graduating from law school in 1982, he became an assistant district attorney in Queens. In 1985, he won a seat as a New York state senator, becoming the youngest ever—he was 31. From then until 2006, Paterson worked

of Massachusetts Republicans to vote against their own party. His victory ended the four-term streak of Massachusetts Republican governors. Once he took office, one of his first goals was to increase state aid to education. He also worked to

*David Paterson, shown here being sworn in as governor, served between 2008 and 2010.*

diligently to serve the people of New York. In 2003, he became the first black leader of the minority party there. Eliot Spitzer chose Paterson as his running mate for the governorship in 2006. The two won in a landslide, and in 2007, Paterson became the first African American lieutenant governor of New York.

When Spitzer resigned in 2008 due to a personal scandal, Paterson became governor. He served out the term until 2010, but he did not seek reelection.

## Black Governors of the Virgin Islands

In addition to governorships of American states, there have been African Americans in high positions in the U.S. Virgin Islands. The United States bought the islands of St. Croix, St. Thomas, and St. John from Denmark in 1917 and named the territory the United States Virgin Islands. Its residents are considered citizens of the United States, and for the last few decades, they have elected their own governor. Before that, governors were appointed. Because the islands are not technically a state, they cannot vote in U.S. federal elections. Since the islands became a U.S. territory, a number of their governors have been black.

William Henry Hastie of Tennessee first worked for the Department of the Interior, where, in 1933, he wrote the constitution for the U.S. Virgin Islands. In 1946, President Harry Truman appointed him governor. He was the first African American to become the governor of a U.S. territory, a position he held until 1949.

President Dwight D. Eisenhower appointed Archie Alphonso Alexander, born in Iowa, to the post of governor in 1954, but he resigned in 1955 after heavy criticism for business conflicts. Eisenhower then appointed Walter Arthur Gordon of Georgia to the position. He served until 1958, when he was appointed federal judge of the District Court of the Virgin Islands.

Melvin Herbert Evans, a native of the island of St. Croix, was appointed to be governor of the islands in 1969. When the territory allowed the residents to vote in a general election to pick their own governor in 1970,

Evans became the first elected governor. In 1978, Evans was elected to the U.S. House of Representatives and then served as ambassador to Trinidad and Tobago in 1981.

Cyril Emmanuel King was also born in St. Croix. After serving in the armed forces in World War II, he completed his education at American University in Washington, D.C. He then worked as an aide in Senator Hubert Humphrey's office, the first black man to serve as an employee in a senator's office. After that, King worked on a committee that amended the first U.S. Virgin Islands constitution. In 1971, President John F. Kennedy appointed him secretary of the islands, which was the equivalent of lieutenant governor. In 1972, he was elected to the Virgin Islands Senate. In 1974, he was elected governor of the U.S. Virgin Islands. He served until his death in 1978.

Most of the recent governors of the U.S. Virgin Islands have been native-born to the territory. Alexander Farrelly—from St. Croix—served as governor from 1987 until 1995. He is credited with making improvements in the infrastructure, ports, and harbors of the territory. Roy Lester Schneider was born in St. Thomas and was a physician in addition to a decorated Vietnam War hero. He

# A POWERFUL NATIONAL IMPACT

In 1989, Wisconsin state representative Annette "Polly" Williams proposed a voucher program to give low-income families state funds so they could enroll their children in private schools. "My fight is for our, for my black children," Williams said in defense of her proposal, "to be able to access this [school] system and get the best that this system offers."[1]

The legislature approved the program, but Williams's idea quickly spread far beyond her home state. The nation's first school choice program ignited a nationwide movement to allow families more power in choosing schools for their children.

Other states followed, and by 2017, 27 states had enacted some type of voucher program. Students are eligible for a range of reasons, including low income, disability, or attending a low-performing school. Research on the effectiveness of voucher programs varies, and there are no clear answers as to whether voucher programs are good or bad for education.

1. Quoted in Bret Lemoine, "Former Wisconsin Rep. Annette 'Polly' Williams, Mother of 'School Choice' Passes Away at 77," Fox News, November 9, 2014. fox6now.com/2014/11/09/former-wisconsin-rep-annette-polly-williams-mother-of-school-choice-passes-away-at-77/.

held the office of governor from 1995 until 1999. During that time, he helped make significant advances in health care.

Charles Turnbull was also born in St. Thomas and followed Schneider in 1999, serving two terms until 2007. His priorities were education and historical and cultural awareness. He received several awards for his efforts. John de Jongh Jr. held the office from 2007 until 2015. He made advances in the uses of renewable energy and also improved early childhood education. De Jongh is also a native of St. Thomas.

Born in Brooklyn, New York, and first serving as a senator and then as lieutenant governor under Schneider, Kenneth Mapp won the gubernatorial election in 2014. His administration focused on adding government jobs and improving the economy.

## Black State Legislators

In addition to the highest role in state government—a governorship—there have been hundreds of elected

# A CAREER OF FIRSTS

Few black public officials have recorded more firsts than Vel Phillips, who was active throughout the mid-to-late 20th century. She was widely loved and supported all throughout her home state of Wisconsin, and the Wisconsin Historical Society wrote about her long and successful career:

> Active in the women's movement and the civil rights movement, Vel Phillips built a career full of "firsts" as both a woman and an African American in Wisconsin ... She ... studied law at the University of Wisconsin-Madison Law School, where in 1951 she became the first African-American woman to graduate from the law school ... In 1956 Phillips became the first woman and the first African-American alder in Milwaukee ... [She was] the first African-American judge in Wisconsin ... In 1978 Phillips made national history as the first woman and first African American elected secretary of state in Wisconsin ... Although Phillips lost the next election, she remained the highest-ranking woman to win state office in the 20th century.[1]

1. Wisconsin Historical Society, "Vel Phillips Receives 2006 'Robert and Belle Case La Follette Award for Distinction in Public Service," Wisconsin Historical Society. www.wisconsinhistory.org/Content.aspx?dsNav=N:4294963828-4294963805&dsRecordDetails=R:CS542.

or appointed African Americans in other state roles. Black influence in California government, for example, increased in 1974, when Mervyn Dymally was elected lieutenant governor, the first African American to hold a statewide office in California. Dymally went on to serve in the U.S. House of Representatives in 1981.

Willie L. Brown Jr. represented San Francisco in the California State Assembly for three decades, and from 1980 to 1995, he was assembly speaker. By controlling the legislature, Brown became one of the most influential political figures the state had ever known. In 1996, he shifted to local government and served as mayor of San Francisco until 2004.

In Georgia, another powerful state legislator, Charles Walker,

*In 1971, Vel Phillips (right) became the first black judge in Wisconsin.*

became majority leader in the State Senate in 1996. In 2017, Nevada's state legislature swore in its first African American assembly speaker, Jason Frierson. Nevada's history of empowering black politicians stretches back to the 1960s. Woodrow Wilson, not to be confused with the former president, became Nevada's first black legislator when he was elected to the assembly in 1966, and Joe Neal became Nevada's first black state senator in 1972. In 2002, Neal, who served as a state senator until 2004, explained why Nevada voters were electing so many African Americans:

*There has been a change. If you meet the voters and explain the issues to them and they are affected by those issues, then they will vote for you. You just have to get out and let people know who you are ... People seem to have gained a liking to black elected officials. They aren't afraid to vote for them.*[37]

By 2010, there were hundreds of African Americans serving in state legislatures. Even states with small black populations still elected a number of black lawmakers. Unfortunately, although progress has been made, it does not seem to be steady. A 2015 survey by the National Conference of State Legislatures and the Pew Charitable Trusts showed that while African Americans account for 13 percent of the U.S. population, only 9 percent of the state legislators are black. In addition, black women have an even lower presence than black men; Georgia and Maryland claim the highest percentages of black female legislators, while Mississippi and Louisiana have the lowest.

## Gains in State Elections

While African American legislators have had an uneven history, other positions in state government have been opened to them. In 1959, Otis M. Smith was elected Michigan's auditor general to become the first African American to win a state-wide election since Reconstruction. In 1963, two more black politicians won statewide office—Gerald Lamb as treasurer in Connecticut and Edward Brooke as attorney general in Massachusetts. In 1978, Vel Phillips, the first female African American city councilor for Milwaukee and Wisconsin's first black judge, was elected Wisconsin's secretary of state. She was Wisconsin's first black statewide constitutional official.

In 2006, Anthony Brown was elected lieutenant governor of Maryland, and five other African Americans were reelected to state-wide offices they already held: New York Lieutenant Governor Paterson, Georgia Attorney General Thurbert Baker, Illinois Secretary of State Jesse White, Connecticut Treasurer Denise Nappier, and Georgia Commissioner of Labor Michael Thurmond.

Nappier was already accustomed to the challenges of her job because she had been Connecticut treasurer since 1999. One of the causes Nappier has championed is affordable housing. Advocating for low-income families in her state has made her popular with all races. Like other politicians before her, she focused on issues that can affect everyone.

In the South, North Carolina has

seen steady diversification over the last few decades. In 1969, Henry Frye was the only African American member of the state House of Representatives, and there were no black senators. Ten years later, there were two senators and three additional House members along with Frye in North Carolina. In 1989, there were 5 black senators and 14 members of the House. The number increased to 7 senators and 19 House members in 1999. The year 2009 saw 10 senators and 23 House members, and by 2017, the numbers had increased by one member in each branch. All of the elected African American officials in this state were Democrats.

*Denise Nappier made a name for herself in state government by improving the lives of low-income families in Connecticut.*

# CHAPTER FIVE
# THE WHITE HOUSE AND CAPITOL HILL

On January 20, 2009, Barack Obama made history when he took the oath of office as president of the United States. Obama was the first African American president. The crowd of nearly 2 million people was the largest crowd for any event ever held in the District of Columbia, as well as the largest presidential inauguration crowd on record. During Obama's first term, there were more than 40 African American congressmen and one senator in the federal government.

In his inauguration speech, President Obama acknowledged the struggles of African Americans over the years. He held out hope that "the old hatreds shall someday pass."[38] Emotionally, he stated that "a man whose father less than sixty years ago might not have been served at a local restaurant can now stand before you to take a most sacred Oath."[39] This inaugural event was one of the most important racial barrier breakdowns in American history.

The 2013 inauguration for President Obama's second term in office was attended by about 1 million people. Despite pushing for racial progress, Obama's second term saw the same number of African American members of Congress. However, three black senators—Cory Booker of New Jersey, William Cowan of Massachusetts, and Tim Scott of South Carolina—represented the largest number of black senators to ever serve at the same time.

The election of President Barack Obama and the increasing number of African Americans in Congress showed how much black political strength had grown since the early 20th century.

*When Barack Obama took the oath of office in 2009, he was breaking down hundreds of years of prejudiced racial barriers in America.*

## A Slow, Steady Increase

On November 6, 1928, Oscar De Priest of Illinois became the first African American elected from a northern state and the first black member of the House of Representatives since North Carolina's George Henry White in 1901. De Priest was also the last African American Republican congressman until Gary Franks of Connecticut in 1990. During the 1920s, a huge portion of black voters switched their allegiance to the Democratic Party because President Franklin D. Roosevelt's social welfare policies helped them and because the Democratic Party began catering more to issues impacting African American communities.

William Dawson of Illinois was elected to the House in 1943. The House finally had two active black members when Adam Clayton Powell of New York was elected in 1945. However, no black senators were elected until 1967. The handful of African American congressmen faced discrimination in Washington. De Priest fought to allow all blacks to eat at the congressional restaurant, claiming that "If we allow segregation and the denial of constitutional rights under the Dome of the Capitol, where in God's name will [African Americans] get them?"[40] Despite his powerful argument, congressional committees refused to overturn the racist policy.

Even in the 1940s, African American legislators faced discrimination. However, they had much more political power. In 1946, for example, Powell made his legislative mark in Congress when he introduced the Powell Amendment to a spending bill. The rule forced companies with federal contracts to practice fair and unbiased hiring practices for minorities, especially African Americans. Powell added similar measures to bills for the next 20 years. In arguing his position, he wrote, "The black masses must demand and refuse to accept nothing less than that proportionate share of political jobs and appointments which are equal to their proportion of the population."[41]

Watching influential African Americans achieve success in Washington, dozens of black politicians ran in—and won—elections during the middle of the 20th century. The number of black members of the House grew steadily from the 1960s onward. In 1993, the House had 40 black members. Representative Edolphus Towns of New York claimed that the increase was "clear evidence of the enhanced power and political influence of African-Americans."[42] That same year, Carol Moseley Braun became the first black woman to serve in the Senate—she was also the only black senator during her term. By 2003, there were 39 African American members of the House, but none in the Senate. The 115th Congress (2017–2019) reached new highs with 49 black members of Congress; Mia Love of Utah was the only Republican. Of the three senators—Cory Booker, Kamala Harris, and Tim Scott—only Scott was a Republican.

## Elected by Popular Vote

Edward W. Brooke was born on October 26, 1919, in Washington, D.C. Brooke, whose father was a lawyer for the federal Veterans Administration, has admitted that his early life was not defined by

# THE CONGRESSIONAL BLACK CAUCUS

With the number of African American members of Congress at an all-time high of 13 in 1971, they saw a need for a structured, nonpartisan group to advance the interests of African Americans. All 13 congresspeople formed the Congressional Black Caucus (CBC). Charles Rangel named the group, which worked as a single, powerful unit to support legislation that would benefit blacks across the nation. One of their early victories came when they boycotted President Richard Nixon's State of the Union address because he had refused to meet with them. Later, Nixon did host a meeting.

One major success for the CBC was having the third Monday in January designated as an official government holiday in honor of Martin Luther King Jr. Over the years, the CBC has addressed issues such as taxation, social justice, voting rights, health care, jobs, economic opportunity, law enforcement, and free speech. By the 115th Congress (2017–2019), the group had 49 total members who served millions of citizens.

*The Congressional Black Caucus is shown here meeting with Melvin Van Peebles, an influential black filmmaker.*

*Edward Brooke was one of the most influential African American senators of all time. He paved the way for future federal officials in America.*

His political independence and his fine work on other issues impressed Massachusetts's voters. Just four years after achieving his first elected office, on November 8, 1966, his state elected him to be a federal senator. Brooke was the first African American in history to be elected to the Senate by popular vote.

In the Senate, he voted against three people Republican president Richard Nixon nominated for the U.S. Supreme Court because he considered them unfit candidates. He also criticized Nixon for failing to keep his 1968 presidential campaign promise to end the Vietnam War quickly. "I was proud to be a Republican," Brooke once said, "but my ultimate loyalty was to certain goals and ideals, not to party."[43] Brooke served two terms in the Senate before being defeated in 1978.

discrimination and racism. After graduating from Howard University in 1941, Brooke fought in World War II with a segregated black unit in the U.S. Army. After the war, Brooke went to Boston University Law School, settled in Massachusetts, and entered politics as a Republican.

In 1962, he won the election for attorney general of Massachusetts.

# African American Congresswomen

When Carol Moseley Braun took her Senate seat in 1993, she was the first black senator to be elected since Edward Brooke; she was also the only black senator that term. African American women have had more success, however, in the House of Representatives. Many have been Democrats, and most have served several terms: Shirley Chisholm (1969–1983), Corrine Brown (1993–2017), Eva Clayton (1991–2003), Barbara-Rose Collins (1991–1997), Cynthia McKinney (1993–2007), Carrie Meek (1993–2003), Eleanor Holmes Norton (1991–incumbent), and Maxine Waters (1991–incumbent).

In 1997, Congresswoman Carolyn Cheeks Kilpatrick of Detroit explained why the number of black women elected to the House continued to increase: "I think when you have African-American females who have excelled ... we bring such traits as intelligence, hard work, dedication and sensitivity to the people we represent."[44]

The congresswomen of the late 20th century owed part of their success to the first black woman elected to Congress: Representative Shirley Chisholm. Born in Brooklyn, New York, on November 30, 1924, she was elected to the New York state legislature in 1964. Four years later, she defeated civil rights leader James Farmer for a seat in Congress. After her victory, Chisholm, a Democrat, declared, "Just wait, there may be some fireworks."[45] She personally created those fireworks during her 14 years in office by fighting hard to help poor people of all races. Chisholm backed spending increases for education, health care, and minority employment initiatives. She also opposed the Vietnam War and the military draft, which she claimed resulted in a disproportionate number of black men being sent to fight in Vietnam.

She was one of the founding members of the Congressional Black Caucus in 1971. In 1972, Chisholm made history again as the first black woman to campaign for a major party's presidential nomination. Even though she knew she had no chance of winning, Chisholm said she ran because "I want history to remember me ... not as the first black woman to have made a bid for the presidency ... but as a black woman who lived in the 20th century and who dared to be herself. I want to be remembered as a catalyst for change in America."[46]

# *UNBOUGHT AND UNBOSSED*

Shirley Chisholm had to overcome two massive barriers—sexism against women and racism against blacks—to accomplish anything in her life. What makes her remarkable is that she was able to achieve so much despite American prejudices. In her memoir, *Unbought and Unbossed*, she explained the issues facing women in the 20th century:

*Why are women herded into jobs as secretaries, librarians, and teachers and discouraged from being managers, lawyers, doctors, and members of Congress? Because it is assumed that they are different from men. Today's new militant campaigners for women's rights have made the point that for a long time society discriminated against blacks on the same basis: they were different and inferior. The cheerful old darky on the plantation and the happy little homemaker are equally stereotypes drawn by prejudice. White America is beginning to be able to admit that it carries racial prejudice in its heart, and that understanding marks the beginning of the end of racism. But prejudice against women is still acceptable because it is invisible. Few men can be persuaded to believe that it exists. Many women, even, are the same way.*[1]

*Shirley Chisholm was one of the most influential women in the U.S. Congress.*

1. Shirley Chisholm, *Unbought and Unbossed*. Washington, DC: Take Root Media, 2009. PDF e-book.

## A Political Surprise

One of the biggest political surprises of 1992 was Carol Braun's victory in an election for a U.S. Senate seat. The University of Chicago Law School graduate held the low-level position of Cook County recorder of deeds when she challenged Senator Alan Dixon in 1992. Even though Braun had been an Illinois state legislator from 1978 until 1988, she seemed like an underdog against an incumbent senator. She admitted after her election that she knew she was an unlikely candidate: "I was female, working class and black. I joked it was a triple-dose of diversity."[47]

A highlight of her single term came in 1993 when she persuaded the Senate to refuse to renew a patent for the United Daughters of the Confederacy's logo, which included the Confederate flag. In an impassioned speech to her fellow senators, Braun explained that the Confederate flag is a symbol of a racist past:

*I have to tell you this vote is about race. It is about racial*

# PRESIDENTIAL AND VICE PRESIDENTIAL CANDIDATES

The first African American nominated to run for vice president was Frederick Douglass in 1872. He was a former slave who became one of the 19th century's most powerful leaders in the fight for black rights. Douglass never campaigned because the Equal Rights Party chose him without his consent. Senator Blanche Kelso Bruce of Mississippi then received eight votes for vice president at the Republican Party convention in 1880. In 1932, James W. Ford was the first African American on a presidential ticket in the 20th century; he was the Communist Party USA vice presidential candidate.

In 1972, Representative Shirley Chisholm was the first black woman to try to run for president. In addition to Barack Obama, other African American candidates for president have included civil rights leader Jesse Jackson (1984 and 1988), as well as black activist Al Sharpton and former U.S. senator Carol Moseley Braun (2004). Republicans who have campaigned but did not gain much support were: Alan Keyes (1996, 2000, and 2008), Herman Cain (2000 and 2012), and Ben Carson (2016).

*symbolism. It is about racial symbols, the racial past, and the single most painful episode in American history [the Civil War] ... If there is anybody in this chamber, anybody, indeed anybody in this world, that has a doubt that the Confederate effort was around preserving the institution of slavery, I am prepared and I believe history is prepared to dispute them ... Now, to suggest as a matter of revisionist history that this flag is not about slavery flies in the face of history ... It is an outrage. It is an insult. It is absolutely unacceptable to me and to millions of Americans, black or white, that we would put the [approval] of the United States Senate on a symbol of this kind of idea.*[48]

Braun's one term in office was clouded by unproven accusations that she had misused some campaign funds. After her Senate term, President Bill Clinton appointed her as ambassador to New Zealand and Samoa in 1999. In 2003, she campaigned briefly for the Democratic Party's presidential nomination, eventually dropping out and supporting another candidate. After that, Braun started her own organic food company.

## From the Senate Chamber to the Oval Office

The fifth African American senator in U.S. history and the 44th President of the United States was born on August 4, 1961, in Honolulu, Hawaii, to a black father—Barack Obama Sr., a native of Kenya, Africa—and a white mother—Ann Dunham, who was born in Kansas. Barack Obama graduated from Harvard Law School in 1991 and moved to Chicago, where he practiced law and became involved in politics. In 1996, Obama was elected to the Illinois State Senate, where he won praise for helping draft laws on health care and welfare and reducing race-motivated arrests by police. Obama was a candidate for the U.S. Senate when he gave the keynote speech on July 27, 2004, at the Democratic National Convention. The fame Obama received from his speech helped him defeat his two opponents, Blair Hull and Daniel Hynes.

Obama's early accomplishments, engaging personality, and outstanding speaking skills made him a rising star in the Democratic Party. He has often joked about how confused people are that he has a Muslim name despite being a Christian: "Everywhere I went I'd

*President Barack Obama, shown here in 2016, dedicated large parts of his administration to reducing discrimination across the country.*

# FIRST LADY MICHELLE OBAMA

As the nation's first African American First Lady, Michelle Obama took her duties seriously. In 2009, she planted an organic garden on the White House grounds and frequently invited groups of schoolchildren to help with its cultivation. Her Let's Move! program was designed to encourage children and adults to have more active lifestyles. She worked with various organizations to improve the quality and quantity of healthy, nutritious foods available in urban and rural areas where it was scarce. Obama was instrumental in improving school lunch programs nationwide.

Along with Second Lady Dr. Jill Biden, she created Joining Forces to support military families and veterans. Her Let Girls Learn program worked with the president and several government agencies to encourage girls all over the world to pursue their educations.

Obama is considered by many to be a role model who inspired many through her public appearances and speeches during her time as First Lady. She has made many television appearances, including a guest appearance on *Sesame Street*. Obama has maintained several social media accounts, encouraging communication with all of America's diverse groups.

During a speech at the Democratic National Convention in 2012, Obama said, "Every day, the people I meet inspire me ... every day, they make me proud ... Serving as your first lady is an honor and a privilege."[1]

1. Quoted in "Transcript: Michelle Obama's Convention Speech," NPR, September 4, 2012. www.npr.org/2012/09/04/160578836/transcript-michelle-obamas-convention-speech.

get the same ... questions. Where'd you get that funny name, Barack Obama? Although people would mispronounce it. They would call me Alabama, they called me Yo' Mama."[49]

The prominence Obama gained in the Senate led him on to announce his candidacy for president on February 10, 2007. Political analysts claimed he was the first African American to have a legitimate chance to win that office. Their analysis proved correct—Obama won the election on November 3, 2008, after a long and challenging campaign against Senator John McCain. He won nearly 100 percent of the black

*Michelle Obama will be remembered as an advocate for American children.*

vote and also won a large portion of the Latino vote. In 2012, Obama won another hard-fought election, giving him a second term as president. In his acceptance speech, he said he was "more determined and more inspired than ever about the work there is to do and the future that lies ahead."[50]

## A Bright Political Future

The power that African Americans wield in Congress today stands in stark contrast to the long periods in U.S. history during which they had absolutely no say in governing their nation. On July 25, 1974, Representative Barbara Jordan of Texas commented in a speech to the House Judiciary Committee on how black political power was already growing:

> *The Constitution of the United States [begins]: "We, the people." It's a very eloquent beginning. But when that document was completed on the seventeenth of September in 1787, I was not included in that "We, the people." I felt somehow for many years that George Washington and Alexander Hamilton just left me out by mistake. But through the process of amendment, interpretation, and court decision, I have finally been included in "We, the people."*[51]

# CHAPTER SIX
# HIGH-PROFILE APPOINTMENTS

The Appointments Clause of the Constitution grants the president the power to make appointments to certain government positions with the approval of the Senate. Up until the mid-1960s, few black people had received such appointments. President Lyndon B. Johnson broke this racial boundary when he appointed Thurgood Marshall as the first black Supreme Court justice.

The civil rights victories in the 1960s made Marshall's and many following appointments possible. One moment of Condoleezza Rice's childhood illustrated this victory. As a young girl, Rice visited Washington, D.C. with her parents. As they walked past the White House, she said, "Daddy, I'm barred out of there now because of the color of my skin. But one day, I'll be in that house."[52] Rice's

prediction came true when she was sworn in as the first black female secretary of state, serving under President George W. Bush. Her appointment made her one of the most powerful government officials in the country.

Presidents Jimmy Carter, George W. Bush, and Bill Clinton all increased the number of African Americans appointed to their cabinets and other high-level positions in the federal government. When President Obama took office, he raised the number even higher.

Some state and local officials also have the power to make appointments. Since the passage of the Voting Rights Act in 1965, thousands of male and female black officials at all levels of government have been appointed to a wide variety of positions, such as police and fire chiefs, school

*Condoleezza Rice was among the most powerful members of the U.S. government during the administration of President George W. Bush.*

superintendents, and state and federal judges. The Voting Rights Act helped make these appointments possible because it increased the voting power of African Americans. These courageous and talented African Americans served their country well, paving the way for future generations.

## Justice Thurgood Marshall

Thurgood Marshall was born July 2, 1908, in Baltimore, Maryland, and he was subjected to racist treatment throughout his entire life. In 1930, despite strong academic qualifications, the University of Maryland Law School refused to admit him because he was black. That particularly unfair treatment made him so angry that he decided to dedicate his life to fighting for black equality: "They wouldn't let me go to the law school because I was a Negro, and all through law school I decided I'd make them pay for it, and so when I got out and [became a lawyer], I proceeded to make them pay for it."[53]

After graduating from Howard University Law School, Marshall became a civil rights lawyer for the NAACP. His biggest victory was in *Brown v. Board of Education of Topeka*. Marshall argued that the segregated school system in Topeka, Kansas, was illegal because black schools were always inferior to those for whites. In a unanimous 9-0 decision on May 17, 1954, the Court ruled that school segregation was illegal. Marshall was overjoyed with the verdict because Supreme Court decisions have powerful effects on the entire nation. The ruling ended segregated school systems and brought Marshall into the national spotlight for his work.

Marshall went on to serve in the U.S. Court of Appeals and then as solicitor general, the official who represents the nation before the Supreme Court. Marshall won 14 of the 19 cases he argued for the government, more than any other American in history. When President Johnson named Marshall to the high court in 1967, southern senators tried unsuccessfully to block his nomination. The Senate confirmed Marshall on August 30, 1967, and he served with distinction for 24 years, retiring in 1991.

On July 1, 1991, President George H.W. Bush nominated Clarence Thomas to replace Marshall. When Thomas was confirmed on October 15, 1991, he became the nation's second African American Supreme Court justice. Though he was the only black member of the high court serving at the time, lower federal courts were becoming more accepting of black judges nationwide.

## From Few to Many

There were few black judges at any

*George E. C. Hayes (left), Thurgood Marshall (middle), and James M. Nabrit (right)*
*are shown here walking down the steps of the Supreme Court building after the*
Brown v. Board of Education *case that eliminated segregation in American schools.*

# A CORE BELIEF IN THE LAW

Thurgood Marshall was a symbol of greater African American equality in a troubled time for minorities in the United States. However, his life was also inspiring for people of any race who believed in the American dream:

*Thurgood Marshall's is the [essential] American story. Born to a modest, racially mixed and determined family, he rose on the basis of talent and hard work to become the first black justice of the Supreme Court. Most important, of course, he deployed the law like an army to force the United States to live up to the principles on which it was founded. He was [essentially] American because he used his brilliance and his sweat to beat the racist establishment at its own game, defeating it on the very terrain of the law that, until Marshall came along, it had exploited to maintain its [power] ... Marshall's core belief was in the law and in the facts ... In one instance, investigating angry ... accusations that the police had brutally beaten a black woman in New York in 1959, "I sided with the policemen," Marshall [said] years later. His core belief was not the radical one that the law itself is an instrument of white power ... but that it was a neutral instrument that could be put to the task of forcing whites to accept blacks as equals.*[1]

1. Richard Bernstein, "Books of the Times; A Civil Rights Hero Inside the Law," *New York Times*, December 30, 1998. www.nytimes.com/1998/12/30/books/books-of-the-times-a-civil-rights-hero-inside-the-law.html.

level until the early 1850s, when Robert Morris held a low position—magistrate—in several courts in Boston. African American judges remained a rarity for nearly a century after that. In 1939, New York mayor Fiorello La Guardia appointed Jane Bolin to the city's family court, making her the nation's first female African American judge.

There were no black federal judges until 1937 when William Hastie was appointed to the U.S. District Court of the Virgin Islands. The first black federal judge in the continental United States was James B. Parsons,

*In 1939, Justice Jane Bolin was the only black female judge in the country.*

President Obama's judicial appointments were African American, which is the highest percentage in U.S. history to date. By 2015, there were more than 100 black federal judges.

Despite gains in federal appointments, it took a long time for a black judge to sit on a state supreme court. State supreme courts are powerful because they review the decisions of lower state courts, where a huge portion of lawsuits take place. In 1955, Governor W. Averell Harriman named Harold A. Stevens to the New York State Supreme Court, and in 1984, Robert Nelson Cornelius Nix Jr. of Pennsylvania became the first black chief justice of a state supreme court. Leah Ward Sears of Georgia became the first black female to head a state supreme court in 2005. Sears, who began preparing for a career in law at a young age, loved being a judge: "This is what I really always wanted to do, hear the

who on August 9, 1961, became a U.S. district judge in Illinois. There were nearly 70 black federal judges when Parsons retired in 1992. Their numbers swelled under President Bill Clinton, who from 1992 to 2000, appointed 129 judges; nearly 60 percent of those appointments were women or members of minority groups. During his two terms in office, almost 20 percent of

big issues of the day."[54]

By 2010, there were a total of 769 African American justices—378 men and 284 women—serving on state courts. This is the highest number of any ethnic minority group.

Both federally and on a state level, the number of minority judges appointed varies according to the political party in power. According to a Pew Research Center study, from 1940 until 2016, "Democratic presidents have appointed three times as many black judges as their Republican counterparts (162 vs. 49)."[55]

## Other Important African American Positions

In addition to federal judges, presidents have the power to appoint people to lead federal agencies, such as the Department of State and the Department of Defense. These important federal officials also become key advisers to the president and are collectively known as the president's cabinet. The first black cabinet member was Robert Weaver. On January 13, 1966, President Johnson named Weaver secretary of the Department of Housing and Urban Development (HUD). Weaver had earned the honor of being the first African American cabinet member through his decades of fighting for equality for blacks, including time spent as chairman of the NAACP and consulting work for President Franklin D. Roosevelt in the 1930s. Johnson also knew Weaver was famous for the calm and confident manner in which he had always battled racism.

William Coleman Jr. became the first black secretary of transportation when President Gerald Ford appointed him in 1975. In 1977, President Jimmy Carter made Patricia Roberts Harris the first black female cabinet member when he named her to lead HUD. Harris went on to become the secretary of health and human services in 1979. President Ronald Reagan appointed Samuel Pierce as secretary of HUD in 1981. President George H.W. Bush appointed Louis Wade Sullivan secretary of health and human services in 1989.

In two terms starting in 1992, Clinton appointed seven black secretaries to his cabinet: Ron Brown (commerce), Mike Espy (agriculture), Hazel O'Leary (energy), Rodney E. Slater (transportation), Alexis Herman (labor), and Jesse Brown and Togo D. West Jr. (veterans affairs). In May 1997, when Herman was sworn in as labor secretary by Vice President Al Gore, she said "[My father] taught me that you have to face adversity. He taught me to stand by my principles. He also taught me how to work within the system for change."[56]

Clinton also named Joycelyn Elders the first black U.S. surgeon general and appointed nine African American presidential assistants. When Clinton left office in January 2001, presidential assistant Ben Johnson boasted, "We were the most diverse White House in the history of the country—and the most successful ... [Clinton] has clearly done more for Black Americans than any other president in history."[57]

During his two terms, President George W. Bush appointed several African Americans to his cabinet. In 2001, Colin Powell became the first African American secretary of state, and Condoleezza Rice became the first African American national security advisor. Ron Paige served as the Department of Education secretary, while Alphonso Jackson took over as HUD secretary. When Powell stepped down as secretary of state, Condoleezza Rice took over.

Obama appointed only one black cabinet member during his first term—Eric Holder, who was the first African American attorney general. During his second term, he appointed more African Americans:

Loretta Lynch (attorney general), Anthony Foxx (secretary of transportation), John King Jr. (secretary of education), and Jeh Johnson (secretary of homeland security).

Donald Trump appointed Ben Carson as HUD secretary in 2017. Carson is a former neurosurgeon who, despite admitting that he had little administrative or political experience, has pledged to both improve housing and manage the federal budget. He was the only African American appointed to the Trump cabinet as of 2017.

## Powell and Rice Face Criticism

On September 11, 2001, the terrorist group al-Qaeda attacked the United States. Powell advised Bush on how to retaliate for the attack, which included invading Afghanistan on October 7, 2001. Powell also played a key role in starting the war against Iraq on March 20, 2003. Powell helped convince the United Nations that Iraq had weapons of mass destruction. Rice, who was then a national security advisor, also supported the claim. Some historians believe Powell did not think Iraq had such weapons but made the claim out of loyalty to the president. When no weapons were found, the Bush administration was

*After Ben Carson was unsuccessful in his 2016 presidential campaign, President Trump appointed him to lead HUD.*

accused of having twisted intelligence to justify the invasion. Much of the criticism fell onto Powell and Rice, as they were among the outspoken supporters of the invasion.

Although the U.S. Senate confirmed Rice's nomination as secretary of state 85-13 on January 26, 2005, she received a large amount of resistance from the senators. The 13 negative votes were the most against a secretary of state nominee since 1825. The senators voted no to show that they were extremely upset about the misleading claims made about Iraqi weapons to justify the war. Although some African Americans also disliked Rice because they opposed the Iraq War, others appreciated her as a black role model. Michele Moore, a senior vice president for the National Urban League, claimed that Rice's mistakes did not, "diminish the fact that she is a history-making figure. She continues to push the boundaries of opportunity for African American women."[58]

## President Obama and Diversity

Expectations were high when the first African American president took office, and Obama generally did not disappoint his supporters. Obama has been credited for having "the most demographically diverse administration in history … The majority of top policy appointments within the executive branch are held by women and minorities for the first time in history."[59]

In an attempt to find minority candidates, the Presidential Personnel Office reached out to historically black colleges and universities as well as other groups and institutions. The Obama

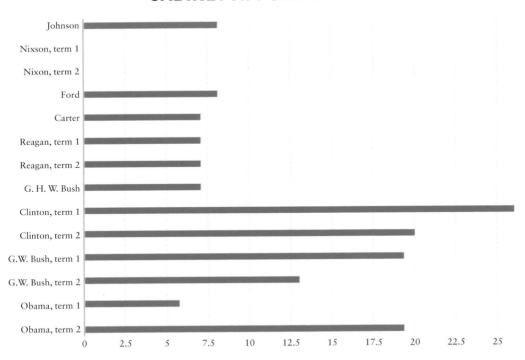

## PERCENTAGE OF AFRICAN AMERICAN CABINET APPOINTMENTS

*This information from the Pew Research Center shows the percentage of African American cabinet appointments from Johnson to Obama.*

administration appointed more than 400 African Americans across all levels of the federal government. These appointments served as a source of pride and encouragement to many in the black community. For many, the ability to work in a presidential administration had never before seemed like a realistic goal.

## Attorneys General Holder and Lynch

President Obama made history when he appointed the first African American attorney general. Eric Holder, who was from New York City, had risen through the political ranks with appointments as an associate judge of the D.C. Superior Court by President Reagan, as a U.S. attorney for Washington, D.C., and as Bill Clinton's assistant attorney general. He also served as a legal advisor for President Obama's first campaign.

Holder was known for successfully

*President Obama appointed the first African American attorney general, Eric Holder, during his first term.*

prosecuting several cases against terrorists, including al-Qaeda associates. He worked with world leaders to reduce the spread of terrorism. Within the United States, Holder supported voting rights for all and criticized the strict voter identification laws that many states were implementing. Holder resigned in 2014 and joined a private law firm. After the Trump administration took office in 2017, Holder began working for the California state legislature.

Loretta Lynch started her legal career in private practice but then went to work for the United States Attorney's Office for the Eastern District of New York. She led that office under President Clinton in 1999, and she did so again under President Obama in 2010. Under her leadership, the office put several terrorists in prison.

When Holder resigned, President Obama appointed Lynch to his position, making her the first African American female attorney general. Lynch made countering terrorism (from both overseas and within the country) and cybersecurity two

of her main priorities. In addition, she focused on reducing gun violence and violence against women. She also continued Holder's work to end voter suppression. At her nomination announcement, she said,

*The Department of Justice is the only Cabinet Department named for an ideal. And this is actually appropriate, because our work is both aspirational, and grounded in gritty reality. It's both ennobling, and it's … profoundly challenging.*

*Today, I stand before you so thrilled, and, frankly, so humbled to have the opportunity to lead this group of wonderful people who work all day and well into the night to make that ideal a … reality, all as part of their steadfast protection of the citizens of this country.*[60]

# CHAPTER SEVEN
# PROGRESS IN SPITE OF RACISM

For the majority of the history of the United States, there were no African Americans in positions of political power. Though the end of the Civil War gave voting rights to African Americans, it took nearly a century for more equal political rights to truly spread. Once black people regained their right to vote nationwide in the 1960s, they not only proved themselves to be informed voters, but also capable government officials. This was especially true in the South, where whites had either forced blacks into slavery or denied them basic rights for centuries. In 2000, Mississippi and Alabama combined had more African American elected officials than there were across the entire nation in 1970. By 2007, there were more than 9,000 black officials in the country, and by 2017, the number was well above 10,000.

Data indicated that more African Americans than whites voted in the 2012 presidential election—the first time in history whites were outnumbered at the polls.

Despite the gains African Americans have made in recent decades, discrimination continues to negatively affect their lives. This is true not only for regular citizens, but also for African Americans elected and appointed to all levels of government positions.

## Harsh Treatment of Black Officials

Even within the government itself, law enforcement officials sometimes treat African Americans more harshly than they do whites. This even happens to prominent black officials, such as former Virginia governor Douglas Wilder. In March 1995, one year after Wilder's term as governor ended, he traveled to North Carolina to speak at Duke University. At the Raleigh-Durham Airport for his return flight home, Wilder was harassed by a white security guard after he set off an airport metal detector. Wilder described what happened: "When I told the White security man that it must be my suspenders [that set off the detector], he literally snapped. He grabbed me, then pushed me and choked me. [It] shouldn't make any difference whether I am a former governor. A human being shouldn't be treated this way."[61]

On March 29, 2006, U.S. Representative Cynthia McKinney of Georgia was involved in a highly publicized incident when a white guard tried to stop her from entering the Capitol. McKinney hit the guard when he grabbed her. Although McKinney was criticized for striking the guard, she claimed "the whole incident was instigated by the inappropriate touching and stopping of me, a female, black congresswoman."[62] Even though McKinney was not wearing a special pin given to members of the House to identify themselves, she said the guard treated her more roughly than the circumstances required—and did so because she was black.

Even the many advances during the Obama administration did not stop racism. Jason R.L. Wallace served as a personal aide to First Lady Michelle Obama for several years. While assisting her at the funeral of former first lady Betty Ford in California in 2011, security identification pins were not available. Despite reassurances from the Secret Service that he would be able to access all areas, local police refused entry to Wallace, but gave access to his white co-workers who also did not have the required identification pins. Wallace reported that the police officers made him wait in the back of a police car. He was eventually able to get in touch with White House officials and was released. The officer who denied him entry was punished, and the Secret Service offered him an apology. Wallace said of the incident: "Even while you're working for the White House, you're still black. You're still black and this stuff still happens."[63]

## Racist Attacks Against Barack Obama

The U.S. Secret Service had to begin protecting Obama before he was elected president because of threats made against him on white supremacist websites and in letters he received. One racist blogger wrote, "Our world will become unbearable with him as President. Maybe there will be someone who would take [a] chance and [assassinate] him? Is that our only hope?"[64] Understandably, national security experts believed posts similar to this were close to direct death threats. Both open and implied threats of violence forced the government to provide security for Obama and his family earlier in a campaign than any candidate who had ever run for president before him.

Racism was also evident in some criticism of Obama, both during his campaign and throughout his presidency. Some whites opposed Obama because they believed no black person was competent enough to be president. Others repeatedly, and incorrectly, claimed he was not a U.S. citizen, pointing out that his father was African. These accusers ignored or disbelieved the fact that his mother was white and that he was born and raised in Hawaii. When such people attacked Obama's positions on issues or statements he had made, they often used racist terms, obscenities, and other offensive

language. During and after his time in office, millions of Americans have refused to acknowledge any of the gains the country made during his presidency. Whatever progress was made was attributed to other politicians, not to him.

The 2012 election highlighted some of the racism in the country, as election results showed that Obama won only 39 percent of the white vote. Still, the high turnout of African American and other minority voters gave him a solid victory. David Axelrod, Obama's senior advisor, commented on the racism the president endured: "It's indisputable that there was a ferocity to the opposition and a lack of respect to him that was a function of race."[65]

During an interview in 2016, President Obama acknowledged the racism that came from both the general population as well as from some politicians, especially those opposed to Democrats. When asked how he felt about his legacy as the first African American president, Obama said he was comfortable: "The concept of race in America is not just genetic … It's cultural, it's this notion of a people who look different than the mainstream, suffering terrible oppression, but somehow being able to make out

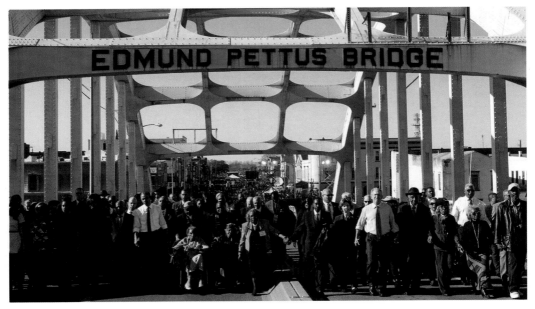

*Barack Obama, Michelle Obama, their daughters Sasha and Malia, members of Congress, and other civil rights leaders walked across the Edmund Pettus Bridge in Selma on March 7, 2015. The walk was in commemoration of the civil rights demonstration there in 1965.*

of that a music, a language and a faith, and a patriotism."[66]

## The Struggle Continues

John Lewis, an icon in the fight for equality for African Americans, has been a member of Congress since 1987. During the 1960s, he was active in the civil rights movement and participated in the freedom ride of 1961 to protest segregated bus terminals. He was arrested more than 40 times and beaten by white police officers more than once. He almost died from head injuries sustained on the march from Selma on March 7, 1965. In spite of adversity, Lewis has continued his work for equality and civil rights throughout his long career in Congress. He has encouraged people to keep fighting to end racism and reach full equality for people of all races in America:

*Our struggle is a struggle to redeem the soul of America. It's not a struggle that lasts for a few days, a few weeks, a few months, of a few years.*

*It is the struggle of a lifetime, more than one lifetime. But I truly believe that one day we will get there, we will arrive. And if we do it right in America, maybe, just maybe, we can serve as a model for the rest of the world.*[67]

# NOTES

## Introduction: From Enslavement to the Presidency

1. Barack Obama, "The Text of Barack Obama's Keynote Address to the 2004 Democratic National Convention," PBS. www.pbs.org/newshour/bb/politics-july-dec04-obama-keynote-dnc/.
2. Obama, "The Text of Barack Obama's Keynote Address."
3. Quoted in Jin-Ping Wu, *Frederick Douglass and the Black Liberation Movement: The North Star of American Blacks*. New York, NY: Garland Publishing, 2000, p. 108.
4. Quoted in "History-maker focuses on future," *Denton Record-Chronicle*, June 27, 2007.

## Chapter One: A New Political Life for African Americans

5. John Mercer Langston, "Citizenship and the Ballot: The Relations of the Colored American to the Government and Its Duty to Him—A Colored American the First Hero of the Revolutionary War," Electronic Oberlin Group. www.oberlin.edu/external/EOG/LangstonSpeeches/citizenship.htm.
6. Quoted in Danielle Alexander, "Forty Acres and a Mule: The Ruined Hope of Reconstruction," *HUMANITIES*, January/February 2004. www.neh.gov/humanities/2004/january-february/feature/forty-acres-and-mule.
7. Quoted in Walter Lynwood Fleming, *The Sequel of Appomattox: A Chronicle of the Reunion of the States*, vol. 32. New Haven, CT: Yale University Press, 1919, p. 230.
8. Quoted Stetson Kennedy, *After Appomattox: How the South Won the War*. Gainesville, FL: University Press of Florida, 1995, p. 75.
9. Quoted in Eric Foner, *Forever Free: The Story of Emancipation and Reconstruction*. New York, NY: Knopf, 2005, p. 128.
10. Quoted in Dorothy Sterling, *The Trouble They Seen: The Story of Reconstruction in the Words of African Americans*. Cambridge, MA: Da Capo Press, 1994, p. 190.
11. Quoted in Lerone Bennett Jr., "The First Black Governor," *Ebony*, November 1986, p. 126.
12. Kwando M. Kinshasa, *African American Chronology: Chronologies of the American Mosaic*. Westport, CT: Greenwood Press, 2006, p. 56.
13. Quoted in George A. Sewell and Margaret L. Dwight, *Mississippi*

*Black History Makers*. Jackson, MS: University Press of Mississippi, 1984, p. 24.

14. Quoted in Dorothy Sterling, *The Trouble They Seen*, p. 178.

## Chapter Two: Political Power Is Lost and Regained

15. Quoted in Vincent Harding, *There Is a River: The Black Struggle for Freedom in America*. San Diego, CA: Harvest, 1981, p. 311.

16. Quoted in "A Ku Klux Klan threat, 1868," The Gilder Lehrman Institute of American History. www.gilderlehrman.org/history-by-era/reconstruction/resources/ku-klux-klan-threat-1868.

17. Quoted in Randall Kennedy, *The Persistence of the Color Line: Racial Politics and the Obama Presidency*. New York, NY: Vintage, 2011, pp. 48–49.

18. Quoted in W.E.B. Du Bois, *Black Reconstruction in America 1860–1880*. New York, NY: The Free Press, 1998, p. 193.

19. Quoted in Rayford W. Logan, *The Betrayal of the Negro: From Rutherford B. Hayes to Woodrow Wilson*. New York, NY: Da Capo Press, 1997, p. 15.

20. Quoted in Laughlin McDonald, *A Voting Rights Odyssey: Black Enfranchisement in Georgia*. Cambridge, UK: Cambridge University Press, 2003, pp. 35–36.

21. Quoted in Sheila Smith McKoy, *When Whites Riot: Writing Race and Violence in American and South African Cultures*. Madison, WI: University of Wisconsin Press, 2001, p. 48.

22. Quoted in Quintard Taylor, *In Search of the Racial Frontier: African Americans in the American West 1528–1990*. New York, NY: W.W. Norton & Co., 1998, p. 145.

23. Martin Luther King Jr., "I Have a Dream," The Avalon Project. avalon.law.yale.edu/20th_century/mlk01.asp.

## Chapter Three: African Americans in Local Government

24. Quoted in David R. Colburn, "Running for Office: African-American Mayors from 1967 to 1996" in *African-American Mayors: Race, Politics, and the American City*, David R. Colburn and Jeffrey S. Alder, eds. Urbana, IL: University of Illinois Press, 2001, p. 30.

25. Quoted in Bob Sipchen, "The Riots Behind US, Let the Debates Begin," *Los Angeles Times*, May 7, 1992. articles.latimes.com/1992-05-07/news/vw-2252_1_riot-coverage/2.

26. Quoted in "James C. Hayes: Alaska's First Black Mayor," *Ebony*, October 1993, p. 65.

27. Quoted in LeGina Adams, "Look who's runnin' things," *Black Enterprise* vol. 31 no. 12, July 2001.

28. Quoted in "Introducing: Ron Kirk: First Black Mayor of Dallas," *Ebony*, September 1995, p. 34.

29. Quoted in Tammy Joyner, "Fayetteville's first black mayor is 'bridge-builder,'" *Atlanta Journal-Constitution*, November 7, 2015. www.myajc.com/news/local-govt--politics/fayetteville-first-black-mayor-bridge-builder/Bndk1VDee9jSrgOkdBqe3J/.

30. Quoted in Mellisa Blackburn, "Champion of Freedom," *The Metropolitan*, vol. 29 no. 19, February 1, 2007, p. 14.

## Chapter Four: Black Politicians in States and Territories

31. Quoted in B. Drummond Ayres Jr., "Praising 'New Mainstream,' Wilder Takes Virginia Oath," *New York Times*, January 14, 1990. www.nytimes.com/1990/01/14/us/praising-new-mainstream-wilder-takes-virginia-oath.html.

32. Cecil Partee, interview by Illinois General Assembly Legislative Research Unit, *First Reading*, vol. 19 no. 3, February 2006, p. 2. www.ilga.gov/commission/lru/feb-2006firstrdg.pdf.

33. Quoted in Donald P. Baker, "Roots of Wilder Victory," *Washington Post*, November 7, 1985. www.washingtonpost.com/archive/politics/1985/11/07/roots-of-wilder-victory/ce3ac6d6-39e8-4f84-a188-4ed767c6d4ef/?utm_term=.46c77195da72.

34. Quoted in Michael Oreskies, "Joy of Democrats Diluted in Virginia," *New York Times*, November 9, 1989. www.nytimes.com/1989/11/09/us/the-1989-elections-virginia-joy-of-democrats-diluted-in-virginia.html.

35. Quoted in Carolyn Click, "Wilder withdraws from Democratic presidential campaign," *United Press International*, January 8, 1992. www.upi.com/Archives/1992/01/08/Wilder-withdraws-from-Democratic-presidential-campaign/8680694846800/.

36. Deval Patrick, "Have Americans Forgotten Who They Are?," *Los Angeles Times*, September 2, 1996. articles.latimes.com/1996-09-02/local/me-39898_1_african-american.

37. Quoted in Ed Vogel, "Election victories: Black legislators overcome odds," *Las Vegas Review-Journal*, December 23, 2002.

## Chapter Five: The White House and Capitol Hill

38. Barack Obama, "First Presidential

Inaugural Address," delivered January 20, 2009, Washington, DC. American Rhetoric. www.americanrhetoric.com/speeches/barackobama/barackobamainauguraladdress.htm.

39. Obama, "First Presidential Inaugural Address."

40. Quoted in "Representative Oscar De Priest of Illinois and the Members' Dining Room," History, Art & Archives, U.S. House of Representatives. history.house.gov/HistoricalHighlight/Detail/35119?ret=True.

41. Quoted in "Powell's 'Black Position Paper' Cites Nineteen Black 'Musts,'" *Jet*, April 7, 1966, p. 6.

42. Quoted in "40 Blacks Now In Congress Can Help Blacks Get Ahead," *Jet*, November 23, 1992, p. 16.

43. Quoted in Kenneth J. Cooper, "First Black Senator Elected By Popular Vote Tells His Story," *The Crisis*, January–February 2007, p. 47.

44. Quoted in Lisa Jones Townsel, "Sisters in Congress prove they have what it takes to bring about change," *Ebony*, March 1997, p. 40.

45. Quoted in Scott Crass, *Statesmen and Mischief Makers: Officeholders Who Were Footnotes in the Developments of History From Kennedy to Reagan*. Xlibris, 2015. PDF e-book.

46. Quoted in Jackson Landers, "When Shirley Chisholm Ran for President, Few Would say: 'I'm With Her,'" *Smithsonian*, April 25, 2016. www.smithsonian-mag.com/smithsonian-institution/when-shirley-chisholm-ran-for-president-few-would-say-im-with-her-180958699/.

47. Quoted in Eric L. Smith, "Changing of the Guard: Carol Moseley-Braun loses bid at second term in Senate," *Black Enterprise*, January 1, 2000. www.blackenterprise.com/mag/changing-of-the-guard-3/.

48. Quoted in Ashlyn K. Kuersten, *Women and the Law: Leaders, Cases, and Documents*. Santa Barbara, CA: ABC-CLIO, 2003, pp. 216–217.

49. Quoted in Larissa MacFarquhar, "The Concilator: Where is Barack Obama coming from?," *New Yorker*, May 7, 2007. www.newyorker.com/magazine/2007/05/07/the-conciliator.

50. Quoted in "Audio And Transcript: Obama's Victory Speech," NPR, November 7, 2012. www.npr.org/2012/11/06/164540079/transcript-president-obamas-victory-speech.

51. Barbara Charline Jordan, "Statement on the Articles of Impeachment," delivered July 25, 1974, Washington, DC. American Rhetoric. www.americanrhetoric.com/speeches/barbarajordanjudiciarystatement.htm.

## Chapter Six:
## High-Profile Appointments

52. Quoted in Antonia Felix, *Condi: The Condoleezza Rice Story*. New York, NY: Threshold Editions, 2002, p. 1.

53. Quoted in Stuart Taylor, "Marshall Puts Reagan at 'Bottom' Among Presidents on Civil Rights," *New York Times*, September 9, 1987. www.nytimes.com/1987/09/09/us/marshall-puts-reagan-at-bottom-among-presidents-on-civil-rights.html.

54. Quoted in Katheryn Hayes Tucker, "Making History," *Georgia Trend*, June 2005. www.georgiatrend.com/June-2005/Making-History/.

55. Quoted in Sara Atske, "More minority federal judges have been appointed under Democratic than Republican presidents," Pew Research Center, July 19, 2016. www.pewresearch.org/fact-tank/2016/07/19/more-minority-federal-judges-have-been-appointed-under-democratic-than-republican-presidents/.

56. Quoted in "First Black Labor Secretary Alexis Herman Recalls She Learned Perseverance From Her Father," *Jet*, May 26, 1997, p. 5.

57. Quoted in "Highlights of Blacks and the Clinton Years 1992–2001," *Jet*, February 5, 2001, pp. 18, 52.

58. Quoted in Michael H. Cottman and Anne Gearan, "Love Her of Leave Her, Condi Rice Still Does Black Women Proud," AfricanAmerica.org, February 9, 2005. www.africanamerica.org/topic/is-rice-a-neo-tom?reply=128788938051517337.

59. Juliet Eilperin, "Obama has vastly changed the face of the federal bureaucracy," *Washington Post*, September 20, 2015. www.washingtonpost.com/politics/obama-has-vastly-changed-the-face-of-the-federal-bureaucracy/2015/09/20/73ef803a-5631-11e5-abe9-27d53f250b11_story.html?utm_term=.4571c7c0ac4a.

60. Quoted in "Remarks by the President at Nomination of Loretta Lynch for Attorney General," White House, November 9, 2014. obamawhitehouse.archives.gov/the-press-office/2014/11/09/remarks-president-nomination-loretta-lynch-attorney-general.

## Chapter Seven: Progress in Spite of Racism

61. Quoted in Hans J. Massaquoi, "The New Racism," *Ebony*, August 1996, p. 57.

62. Quoted in Associated Press, "McKinney Says Police Officer Touched Her 'Inappropriately,'" *Washington Post*, April 1, 2006. www.washingtonpost.com/wp-dyn/content/article/2006/03/31/AR2006033101720.html.

63. Quoted in Hannah Allam, "For Obama's black appointees, a calling that was more than service to country," *McClatchy DC*, January 16, 2017. www.mcclatchydc.com/news/politics-government/whitehouse/article125766414.html.

64. Quoted in Alex Spillius, "Obama gets security help amid plot fears," *Telegraph*, May 5, 2007. www.telegraph.co.uk/news/world-news/1550693/Obama-gets-security-help-amid-plot-fears.html.

65. Quoted in Kevin Liptak, "Obama's candid reflections on race," CNN, December 7, 2016. www.cnn.com/2016/12/07/politics/obama-race-legacy/.

66. Quoted in Kaitlyn D'Onofrio, "Obama: 'Absolutely' Faced Racism in White House," DiversityInc, December 9, 2016. www.diversity-inc.com/news/obama-legacy-cnn/.

67. Quoted in Philip Eil, "John Lewis marches on: 'Our struggle is a struggle to redeem the soul of America,'" *Salon*, August 8, 2016. www.salon.com/2016/08/08/john-lewis-marches-on-our-struggle-is-a-struggle-to-redeem-the-soul-of-america/.

# FOR MORE INFORMATION

## Books

Carey, Charles W., and Liz Sonnebron. *African-American Political Leaders*. New York, NY: Facts on File, 2011.
This book includes biographical sketches of past and current African American political figures, including Cory Booker, Julian Bond, Barack Obama, Maxine Waters, and Douglas Wilder.

D'Orio, Wayne. *Carol Moseley-Braun: Politician and Attorney*. New York, NY: Chelsea House, 2014.
This biography outlines the life and career of the first African American female senator, who served from 1992 until 1998.

Hill, Marc Lamont, Mary Main, and Cathy Thomason. *African Americans in Law and Politics*. Broomall, PA: Mason Crest, 2012.
This collection includes descriptions of the progress and achievements of African Americans from Reconstruction through the election of President Barack Obama.

Rummel, Jack and G.S. Prentzas. *African-American Social Leaders and Activists*. New York, NY: Facts on File: 2011.
This book has biographical entries of prominent African Americans, including Mary McLeod Bethune, Jesse Jackson, Thurgood Marshall, and Rosa Parks.

Smith, Jessie Carney. *The Handy African American History Answer Book*. Detroit, MI: Visible Ink Press, 2014.
The book is written in a question and answer format, covering a wide range of topics, including civil rights, education, politics, and government.

## Websites

**Black Americans in Congress (history.house.gov/ Exhibitions-and- Publications/BAIC/Black- Americans-in-Congress/)**
This U.S. federal government website includes histories and biographies of African American members of Congress.

**Black Political Participation in Reconstruction (www.gilderlehrman.org/ history-by-era/reconstruc- tion/timeline-terms/black- political-participation-recon- struction)**
This website includes links to essays, primary sources, and multimedia content related to the role of black people in poli- tics during Reconstruction.

**The Civil Rights Era (memory.loc.gov/ammem/ aaohtml/exhibit/aopart9. html)**
This Library of Congress website chronicles the Civil Rights movement from 1948 through 1965, using pictures and primary source documents.

**"Sky's the Limit: Here Are 9 Black Politicians Who Went to HBCUs" (newsone.com/3302712/skys- the-limit-here-are-9-black- politicians-who-went-to- hbcus/)**
This detailed article gives information about prominent politicians who graduated from historically black colleges and universities (HBCUs).

# INDEX

# PICTURE CREDITS

# ABOUT THE AUTHOR

**Barbara M. Linde** has written over 85 nonfiction books for children and young adults. She enjoys doing research and exploring topics firsthand, including spending time on horse ranches, holding a baby alligator, kayaking through mangrove estuaries, and watching spacecraft launches. Barbara has interviewed many experts, including astronauts, rocket scientists, geologists, historians, roller coaster designers, and military personnel. Some of her titles include: *Rocket Scientists*, *Becoming a Supreme Court Justice*, *Civil Rights Crusaders: Thurgood Marshall*, *Slavery in North America*, and *Heroes of the U. S. Army*. She lives in Yorktown, Virginia with her husband, Jeffrey, and a large personal library.